YOU MAY TALK NOW !

Mary Phil Drennan

Published 1994
by
On Stream Publications Ltd.
Currabaha, Cloghroe,
Blarney, Co. Cork,
Ireland.
Tel/Fax 021 385798

ISBN: 1 897 685 94 7

CONTENTS

To the girls in the orphanage who survived with me and in memory of those who didn't

Foreword

On my return to Ireland in 1988 I made contact with some of the past pupils of the Cobh orphanage. I was distressed with what I saw. Loneliness, fear and a dependence on psychiatric help were the hallmarks of the lives many of them were leading. I wanted to comfort them about their troubled past. I couldn't. Maybe when they read this book it will make them and the countless girls and boys who went through similar systems to realise they are not alone.

It is very easy for a psychiatrist to prescribe medication for depression. It is no good if their patients cannot open up and talk about the experiences which are limiting their expression. I hope my book will encourage those who have been afraid up to now to come forward and talk now.

Mary Phil Drennan

She stamped up the wooden stairs and you knew someone was going to get it. I knew it was me because that day I was given charge of a two year-old little girl who fell out of my arms onto the floor. She had no injuries but she had cried a lot. It happened early in the afternoon and the matron had heard the child crying. For punishment I was sent into the cloakroom and told to stay there. My fear was that I would be forgotten and yet I hoped I would be. I stayed there through supper and when the others were going up the stairs to bed at half past eight I sneaked out and went with them. No-one seemed to remember I was supposed to stay in the cloakroom. I should have known better, I had been in the orphanage for nine years.

At ten o'clock I heard the sharp echo of the Scholl sandals on the stairs. Suddenly my bedclothes were pulled back and I felt the chill of the night air on my bare bottom. Matron thrashed the backside off me with a wooden spoon while one of the older girls held my legs down. I can still remember the pain, embarrassment and fear. I experienced that fear over and over again in the seventeen years I was in the orphanage which was my home.

Who am I? What am I? You have a yellow streak in you! You are nobody! You will be just like your mother! You're a bad egg! You'll never be any good! I was to hear these insults repeated constantly as I grew from a child into a woman.

I spent nights crying in bed wondering where I came from and hoping someone would come for me.

CHAPTER 1

†††

The early years

I was put into the orphanage in Cobh County Cork in 1954 at the age of eight months. I had been born in St. Finbarr's Hospital and christened Mary Philomena Drennan. I think I spent the first seven months with my mother at the Legion of Mary hostel on the Mardyke in Cork city. The nuns in Cobh told me later that my mother had been brought to the hostel when I was born. They said she had been 'working' on the quays with the sailors and was picked up when they saw her with a baby under her arm. I have never known my father and am still trying to trace him.

My first memory of the orphanage is standing in the playpen, holding on to the bars, and banging it against the radiator. The room I was in was called Prague, and had a statue of the Infant of Prague on a window sill. This room was the Head Nun's office and I can still picture her writing in big books and answering the black telephone. Sometimes another nun would come into the room and come over and smile at me. I can't remember ever being picked up and cuddled by anyone though it's possible that someone did. I was the only baby in the orphanage at that time and later I remember being joined in the playpen by another younger baby.

Soon I graduated into a high chair in the kitchen where I first met Sister Ita, who was to become my favourite nun. I sat in the dark wooden chair for hours and hours watching her stirring pots and rolling out enormous white sheets of pastry and lifting them on to long black baking sheets. She would peel and slice the apples straight onto the pastry. She often gave me a slice of apple dipped in sugar and I would lick off the sugar and throw the apple onto the floor. The high chair had a lid which allowed a potty to be inserted. I would sit on the potty for what seemed like hours until I produced the required result. Later I remember seeing the bottoms of younger children with a red ring from sitting for too long. It was Sister Ita who told me that I had cried for three days and three nights when I first came to Cobh.

The nursery held about eight children under the age of seven. It had blue walls with pictures of animals and fairies and the floor had patterned lino. There was a window at one end towards a corner and at the other end was a door and a tall cupboard. There was one armchair for whoever was looking after us and we sat in little chairs with a table in the middle. I loved these chairs. You could rub the palm of your hand on the corner of the seat until a blister was formed. The blister was sore but you waited for it to go and then did it again. Also they were good for rocking and we all rocked backwards and forwards for hours and hours.

The girl in charge of us was quite nice and I don't ever remember any nastiness about her. She would take oranges from a round tin and divide them between us. In the corner of the room was the Pot-Chair which we used as a toilet. If we had ringworm we had to sit on this chair with the lid down; I remember a lot of children having ringworm on their bottoms (including myself). There was feeling of security in the nursery. We had toys and played games, coloured in pictures and did lots of drawing and we slept in small dormitories supervised by the same girl.

The coal house was one of my dreads. It was a place you were sent if you were bold. It stood next to the nursery and had no windows, just a big iron door with a huge bolt on the outside. It was pitch black inside with coal heaped up with just enough room to stand inside the door. You couldn't move around because if you stood on a piece of coal, it would loosen other pieces and they would come tumbling down on top of your shoes. I was dragged in there as punishment a few times for reasons I can't remember. What I do remember is the crashing of the bolt across the door, final and uncertain. I remember hearing the others screaming when it was their punishment and I screamed too, hoping that someone would let me out. I never knew how long I would be left there, no-one ever seemed to hear me; if they did they never talked to me or tried to get me out. It seemed like hours.

CHAPTER 2
†††
MY MOTHER

The first time I remember meeting my mother was when I was about six years old. I was in the dining room in the basement after supper and Sister came downstairs. I heard her telling the matron that there was someone up in the parlour to see me. The matron asked her who it was and Sister replied "I think it's her mother". Sister took me by the hand upstairs which we made me feel nervous as she only held our hands when she thought we might be afraid. I wondered what she was protecting me from.

The parlour was a room only used for visitors. It smelled of cigarette smoke which to us was a nice smell as we knew there were visitors around. It also meant that Matron was in good humour. I was led into the large room with lovely old-fashioned pictures on the walls. The furniture was highly polished and the chairs were leather. Three people were in the room: my godmother, Miss Bullen, who I knew as she visited me occasionally, and the Southern Health Board Nurse who drove her. In between them sat a huge woman. My Godmother, pointing to the woman beside her, said to me "Do you know who this woman is?" and because I had heard Sister earlier, I said "My Mother". They all sighed encouragingly and watched me. I walked over to her and she sat me on her lap. I kept trying to slide off as I just didn't want to be near her. I didn't like the feeling of being held tightly and I was uncomfortable with this stranger. I walked over to the window and stood chewing a bag of jellybeans. I never saw her again until I was eleven. I heard later that she had worked nearby in the boy's home in Cappoquin for a couple of years around that time.

CHAPTER 3

†††

The Big Girls Dormitory

When the time came to move into the big girls' dormitory life changed for the worst. Gone was the peaceful feeling, the toys and any sense of individuality. The new dormitory was supervised by the matron. She seemed tall to me and was slim with long black hair tied back in a bun. She wore a black crossover apron which had pink and white daisies printed on the material. Underneath she wore a straight tweed skirt and a jumper which was usually blue, her favourite colour. She always wore Scholl sandals indoors with thick stockings with garters just above her knees. When she sat down at the table and crossed her legs we had a fascinating view from another table as we could see the bare skin of her thigh. We never saw anyone's bare skin and the idea of seeing Matron's knickers was always a possibility. She was stern, strict, rarely smiled and was always picking on someone who got the full force of her deep voice. "Where are you going, what are you two talking about?," she would bellow. We would be so scared we would get tongue-tied and that would guarantee a beating. It was either a stick or wooden spoon that she used, and she would flick it on the backs of our legs or the palms of our hands. The first time I remember getting it was when I got a nosebleed and the blood dripped onto the white bib of my dress (it must have been a Sunday). One of the older girls was told to wash it but the stain never left it and I still had to wear it. The beating was one of many I was to get. At the same time I developed a stutter which only materialised when I had to say something to the matron. She would send me outside the door to get my words together and I would rehearse it perfectly and then make a complete mess of it once I saw her. "Excuse me Matron. Sister wants her k-k-k-k-k-k-k-keys". I would have to keep trying to get it right no matter how many times it took, and she would pull my hair every time I got it wrong. The stutter lasted for about two years.

This was not helped by Sister (the head nun) who I had been fond of while I was in the nursery. She was different with the older girls and now I was an older girl. She was small and old and never smiled, and seemed to have a permanent frown on her forehead. Her habit was long and black with a white starched bib and her face seemed to be stuffed inside its white cage. She carried a black leather strap around with her which seemed to be part of her outfit. She had a deep yet whinging voice which she never used unless she was giving out to someone. You knew Sister was coming when you heard the Rosary beads rattling. These hung from a black leather belt and were huge and black and wooden. You could often hear her muttering the Rosary on these beads as she walked around the playground or up and down the Reck room and hallway.

We always knew when there were new arrivals in the home: there would be a strong smell of Jeyes fluid. This was put into the bath for their wash when they arrived and then that smell was replaced with the smell of the nit lotion which was put onto their hair overnight. I always felt sorry for these new arrivals. They would be brought into the Reck where they were stood on a table and stripped down. They were usually crying for their mothers with the matron shouting at them to stop. Their own clothes were taken away never to be seen again and they were put into the bath together. Later you would see them dressed just like us in our black pinafores, dark jumpers (knitted by the older girls) and itchy tweed skirts. I don't remember doing anything to make these new children feel welcome. They just had to fit in with the rest of us and were given their places in the dormitories. From there they made their own way.

We could tell when the inspector was coming from Dublin when the best quilts were put on the beds. These were brightly coloured with a floral pattern, not like the old shabby ones we usually had on the beds. We were all told to smile at him and were lined up to meet him. The good-looking girls were put in the front row along with Sister and Matron's pets. Matron's pets were allowed to grow their hair long and often had ringlets which were put in on a Saturday for Sunday mass. I was one of Sister's pets as I had been in the home since I was a baby, but I got no other privilege than to be in that front row for the inspector. Anyone with glasses or who was fat or had greasy hair or spots was put behind. New toys were put out in the Reck and were put away again as soon as he left. The best china was also put out on the table as if we used it all the time. Once the inspector was gone the old odd cups and saucers were put out again. Another way we knew the inspector was coming was when the door of the bookcase would be unlocked. We would go over to the books and smell their special musty smell. I wanted to read Alice in Wonderland but was always too terrified to ask in case I got a wollop. Once the inspector came the bookcase would be locked again.

There was a room at the top of the house which had four beds. If you had measles or mumps you were put in there until you were cured. No visitors were allowed so you could be alone for a week or two, except for when meals were delivered. Matron would arrive with Bovril and bread which I loved and she seemed quite caring at these times. The bad part was the potty which sat in the middle of the floor and had a strong smell of urine. There was no toilet paper here or in the dormitories. The only toilet paper available to us was cut-up newspaper which we spent hours reading as it was the only time we got a look at news from outside. I would crumple up the newspaper to soften it before I used it. Of course there was a box of toilet tissue in the visitors toilet, which Matron used.

The toilets we had to use were outside in the back yard. One time when my friend Angela was missing (probably in the infirmary) Matron told us she had been bold and had been flushed down the toilet. We all believed her and were afraid to sit on the toilet, or flush it. We looked into the white toilet bowl and could see a grey stain at the bottom which we thought was Angela's face squashed up. When Angela appeared ten days later we were all able to relax on the toilet again.

CHAPTER 4

†††

Christmas in the orphanage

I loved Christmas at the orphanage. It meant excitement, and Sister was kept busy and had little time to bother us. The whole of Christmas Eve was spent cleaning. Everyone had a job to do and the matron was on edge supervising us and making sure the floors were waxed properly. We resented her walking on the floors as we had to do them again. The whole house smelled of polish and disinfectant. When everything was sparkling we put bits of holly over the holy pictures which hung in the hall and some paper decorations were suspended from the ceiling. Lining up at bedtime on Christmas Eve in the Reck I recall looking at the Christmas cards being put in our places on the wooden seating which lined the walls. We all watched eagerly to see if we got any. Some girls got lots of cards, they were lucky. Some girls got one or two and the rest of us got none. The next day after mass we were allowed to open them and, once read, the matron would take them away and they would never be seen again. I remember very little else about those early Christmases except that one time I was given a doll by 'Santa' and when I wanted to take it to bed with me I wasn't allowed by Matron. No toys were allowed upstairs.

CHAPTER 5

†††

HAPPY MEMORIES

A happy memory I have of Cobh was when I made my First Holy Communion. The night before, the four of us were bathed and our hair was washed and heavy metal clips used to make it wavy. This was quite a treat as we were allowed to grow our hair for the year so we would have curls. The rest of the girls had to have their hair cut in the same style with a side crease and a white ribbon catching up a small bunch of hair close to the forehead. As soon as the Holy Communion was over our hair was cut again.

The day of my Holy Communion was special. Our photograph was taken on the steps of the convent by Sister and we were taken to Cobh Cathedral. We carried pretty posies with a candle in the centre which we had to leave on the seat afterwards. I hated leaving the posy behind as it was so beautiful; I would love to have taken it back to the home to keep. We wore white dresses which had been handed down from other girls and we felt wonderful in them. Our white veils floated behind and were attached to hairbands with little flowers stuck on. The whole class went back to the convent for breakfast and I remember that was the first time I ate a boiled egg. Sister showed us how to crack the shell with a spoon and lift off the top. The egg was delicious and I still love boiled eggs. In later years boiled eggs were a Sunday treat (even though they were rock hard). After breakfast we were brought out to the nuns' garden which was full of flowers, mainly roses, and more photographs were taken. Sister Bonaventure gave us a rosary beads each and told us we looked lovely. Angela, from my dormitory, and I spent the rest of the day in Miss Bullen, my Godmother's hostel. With her that day were two women, Nora and Holly, who had huge heads of fuzzy hair. They gave us money and made a fuss of us. The house was full of cats and I made friends with a huge black one.

Miss Bullen gave a statue of Our Lady to Angela and one of the Sacred Heart to me. They were made of plastic and brightly coloured. The figures stood in their own little grotto of see-through white plastic. We were delighted with them as these were ours to keep, unlike our prayer books and Rosary Beads which we never saw again until the day we left the orphanage. From the day of our Communion we had to wear brown scapulas and plastic rosary beads around our necks which often got knotted together. We had to cover the picture on the scapula with a small piece of leather using embroidery thread to protect the picture. We accepted this as something which had to be done, though now it seems ridiculous to have a picture which we weren't allow to see.

CHAPTER 6

†††

My Godmother

My Godmother was a well-spoken, well-educated woman always dressed in a two-piece tweed suit, even in the summer. She always wore a hat, even indoors at home, and she used to come quite often to see us. I say 'us' because there were four other children who were taken into the parlour to see her when she came to the convent. Miss Bullen had been a governess in Finland and now ran a refuge for homeless women in Cork city now known as Edel House. She came to the orphanage about three or four times a year with fruit (usually a bag of oranges) and a box of chocolates for us five girls. We didn't get much benefit from her generosity as we had to hand these to Sister to be divided amongst everyone.

Miss Bullen was one of the privileged visitors who were welcome in the home. She was brought into the parlour and given tea and cake on good china before I was brought in to see her. Not all visitors were as were as welcome as her. My friend Marion's father was never invited inside. Despite the fact that he often helped out with cutting the grass and doing odd jobs, when he visited his daughter he was only allowed to sit on the green bench around the side of the home where Marion was told to meet him. If it was raining he would come to the front door and allowed inside the hall where Marion and her three sisters would be sent to talk to him for just five minutes. He would hand over the usual bags of crisps, thin bars of Cadbury's chocolate and a sixpenny bit for each of them. He would then have to walk the journey back to Cobh in the rain. I felt sorry for him as he seemed old and could have done with a cup of tea. His wife had left him with six children when the youngest was only three and he had no choice but to put them in the orphanage. His treatment as a visitor was even noticeable to us, so he must have felt inferior and sad.

I was lucky to have Miss Bullen visit me as she was always kind and it was good to have someone call to me. I was very fond of her but, because she came to the orphanage as a visitor, I couldn't really get close to her. Sister was always there and we would just talk about how I was doing at school and about the other girls. The occasional time I was alone with her for a few minutes I didn't feel at liberty to ask her anything as we were always very careful about what we said to visitors. In fact we only answered questions, with nothing but the bare essentials. There was so much I wanted to know about myself, but I didn't feel I could ask. I was always afraid she would tell Sister that I was asking questions which I wasn't supposed to know the answers to.

When I left the orphanage many years later I used to ring Miss Bullen and visit her while on holiday from England. She always made me feel welcome with tea and fruitcake and took a great interest in how I was getting on. But still there was a barrier and I never really got to know her before she died in 1980.

CHAPTER 7

†††

The Cobh Orphanage moves to Rushbrooke

The orphanage was attached to Cobh Secondary school, so when the school was due for expansion, we were moved to Rushbrooke, a mile away, to a building which had once been a boarding school.

The week before we moved to Rushbrooke, we slept on mattresses on the floor, as the bases of the beds had already gone out to Rushbrooke. It was great fun sleeping on the floor; we bounced on the mattresses and fooled around a bit as everyone was too busy with packing to notice. As I was only seven and a half years at the time I was very excited, along with the other small girls. I thought that because we were going to a different home, things would be better - no shouting, no getting into trouble and no beatings. The older girls cried as they did not want to move the mile away from the town. They had had the freedom of being sent on errands which would allow them the opportunity to have a look around the town.

I can remember the furniture being carried up the long steps to the back gate and loaded into big Nat Ross vans. We were not used to seeing strangers, particularly men, around the place and this added to the excitement. Even the smell in the orphanage was different, men smoking overtook the scent of polish. All the bigger girls were helping with great enthusiasm, offering to carry boxes and chairs and cushions. Sister came around with a huge can of bullseye sweets and gave them out to everyone helping, including us.

Up to this time I don't remember ever having been to Rushbrooke, so the mile walk was an adventure. There were lots of trees and bushes on the way and seemed very different to the seascape of Cobh. We approached our new home which was surrounded by trees. It all seemed mysterious and I couldn't wait to see what was behind them. The building was smaller than the Cobh one and stood on its own. It was two storeyed and painted grey with white double doors with stained glass panels and had one step in front of the door. It was surrounded by a well-kept lawn with a grassy bank edged with rose bushes.

We went in the gate and were told not to look in the windows and to play around the side, as people were coming into the church, which was part of the building, and peeping out to have a look at the new arrivals - us. I was dying to get into the home to see what it was like, but every time one of us went to the windows Matron told us to go away. The older girls were inside making up the beds and sorting things out. We were called for supper into the kitchen as the dining room was still being decorated. After bread and butter and jam we were led up to the dormitories.

These were large rooms with high ceilings and were much bigger than in Cobh with eighteen beds in each and looking up you could see the bare rafters up high. Each bed had a locker over the bed head and this is where we kept our nylon Sunday knickers which we wrapped in plastic Kelloggs cornflakes bags. We used to book these bags from the cook who saved them for us and wrote our personal numbers on them so no-one could take them. We had been given these numbers when we came into the orphanage and everything we wore or used had this number on it.

The matron came around and told us which bed was ours. We could judge which one would be ours without her telling us as everything was done by age. The first was the youngest, last the eldest. I had bed number two as I was the second youngest in that dormitory. The only place this system wasn't used was in the dining room where sisters were allowed to sit with each other.

As we settled into our new lodgings we discovered that the

larger dormitories were more fun with more girls to chat to, even though talking was forbidden at all times. We just whispered to each other out of earshot of Matron who was never far away. We also liked the new recreation room which was bright and airy with frosted glass windows and a door out to the back yard. We never used that door unless we were told to go out which we would do in single file, lining up before we left the room. There was no such thing as wandering out and taking a walk by ourselves, everything was regimented.

Our new dormitory had new rules: we all had to sleep facing the same way, and if you turned in your sleep, you were accused of talking to the girl in the next bed and told to turn back or woken up, given a thrashing (a good lash with Matron's hand on the bare bottom) and told to face around the right way. Each bed had a curtain which could be pulled around it when it was cold, never for privacy. One night when the curtains were pulled, Matron caught two girls in bed together. This caused a huge commotion and the rest of us were questioned one by one to find out if we had ever gone into someone else's bed. Those of us who owned up were told to confess it to the Parish Priest in the Cathedral the next day. Our encounter had been perfectly innocent, all we were doing was chatting, but the matron could not be questioned or ourselves defended. We were terrified going to the priest about this sin, we didn't know what we had done, but we knew it was something serious. We were called out of class (we were in 2nd year at that stage) and marched by an older girl down to the cathedral to meet the priest at 11 am. We said what the matron told us to which was *"Bless me Father for I have Sinned, I slept with another girl"*. The priest gave us absolution and we returned to school with no further consequences. But we still felt guilty.

There were two chamber pots in each dormitory. These were kept in the middle of the floor on green cloths which we called apartment cloths (I don't know why). We were not allowed to use the two toilets on the corridor; every morning we took turns to empty the potties into a large bucket outside the door and then we took turns to empty the bucket down the shore in the yard. Even at the age of sixteen we had to use the potty and we found it difficult and embarrassing to stoop down, keep our knees covered and then stand up afterwards without knocking it over. It was also embarrassing knowing that you were waking up the others with the noise; we tried squeezing our muscles to make it quiet, but that didn't always work.

It was the early sixties and television was soon to come to Rushbrooke where it was put into The Reck. We were allowed to watch programmes from 8.15 - 8.45 pm and on Sunday afternoons when the nuns from the convent would join us. If anyone on the television programme kissed, Matron made us turn away until it was finished. There were two framed pictures hanging on the wall opposite the television and if you sat on the right chairs you could see the kiss in the reflection on the glass of the picture. We would all run to these two chairs as we all fantasised about David Janssen as Captain Crane in Voyage to the Bottom of the Sea. We all wanted to be kissed by him, and seeing him kiss someone else was nearly as good. Matron never discovered our deception. We never saw the beginning of a programme and rarely managed to see the end. The programmes had always started before we got into The Reck and then at 8.45, no matter what stage the programme was at, we would have to tidy the chairs against the wall and line up at the door. "Stand in rotation!", she would bark and there was no point in arguing for staying on or trying to peep at the television as we walked away.

CHAPTER 8
†††
CHORES

Our chores which were called charges in the new home were allocated to us. Mine was to take charge of Sacred Heart dormitory which was where I slept. Two of us were given the job of cleaning the dormitory every day. The floors were covered with Lino and had to be swept out. We would have to crawl under the high cast-iron beds to sweep and to dust the skirting boards. We had to make sure that no Mollies (fluffs of dust) would be found. On a Saturday morning the beds on one side were pushed to the other and the floors had to be waxed. First we got the black shoe-marks off with steel wool and then we set about polishing. We used melted down church candles and we had to rub it in with newspaper and then buff it with a tweed cloth which we were told had previously been part of dresses worn over twenty years before. We also had to wash the small brown cups in which the wheels of the beds sat. We soaked them in water and then waxed them afterwards until they shone.

There was also Tall Anthony, which was a long broom-handle topped with a strange hairy head. This was for catching cobwebs on the walls and ceilings. If you were in charge of the dormitory it was up to you to make sure there were no lumps and bumps on the beds so if one of the girls didn't make their beds properly you would have to tell them or fix it yourself. Otherwise this would be an excuse for a beating. The beds had three blankets each and two white sheets with a bolster and pillow. This was all covered with a grey-blue cotton bedspread which was tucked in on all sides.

Saturday was the day when the toilets got a special cleaning. We would have to soak up the water in the toilet bowl with a cloth until it was dry and then clean it with Vim until it was white. Sister then inspected it before we were allowed to flush the water into it again. After that we moved onto the kitchen and back hall. The floors had to be scrubbed with boiling water and carbolic soap. Two of us had to kneel on the bare floors, getting our knees soaked and by the time we finished they would be red and sore. I remember some of the girls bathing their swollen knees in warm water and Sister putting brown iodine all over them. The girls would still have to scrub the floors the next Saturday. The back yard had to be swept on Saturdays also. We took this frustrating job in turns. We would sweep up all the leaves and bits of dirt into a pile, but very often the wind would blow it back all at once. We tried using a dustbin lid to keep the rubbish in one place, but it never worked. That job often took hours.

Another job was polishing shoes. This was done every Friday and two of us would work together. One would put the polish on with a hard shoe brush and the other buffed with a soft cloth. The polish was always brown, no matter what the colour of the shoes, and the shoes were often very old as they had been handed down from girls who had left. The insides were often worn away and had the nails coming up through them, in spite of the cobblers best efforts to flatten them. The cobbler came every Thursday and if we wanted our shoes repaired we wore our Sunday shoes for the day. Working in the downstairs cloakroom, the cobbler would put new heels and soles on them, sticking them with a strong-smelling glue which permeated the orphanage on that day.

One of the big girls loved the smell and once picked up a shoe to get more of it. She inhaled the fumes and passed out on the floor. That was well before glue-sniffing was fashionable.

The laundry was another task. This was done by the classes that didn't have a big exam like the Inter and Leaving Cert. Two of us would be kept out of school on a Friday to assist Sister. On the Thursday night we would shred Sunlight soap with a sharp knife into a big metal bath and large kettles of boiling water were added to it until it dissolved. By the next morning it would be a thick paste. This was ladled into a big drum where the water had come to boiling point and the white sheets added. A motor then turned the drum inside its cylinder. After about twenty minutes Sister would press a large red button which caused the machine to stop with a shudder. She would open the drum and a big gush of hot heavy-smelling steam would shoot out. We would pull each heavy boiling hot sheet into a metal bath underneath using our fingers while Sister used a long wooden tongs. When the bath was full we carried it to a deep white ceramic sink full of cold water. They had to be rinsed in this and then moved into the next sink which had more cold water with a 'blue bag' dipped in it. We had to dip them in one at a time reaching up high to make sure the blue rinse was evenly spread. The cold water would go up our sleeves and there was nothing we could do, though Sister had white false elasticated sleeves to stop her from getting wet. Our clothes managed to stay dry as we wore big mackintosh aprons which reached your turned down wellington boots. Next the two of us wrung the sheets which was very difficult as they were so heavy. Not a drop could be left before we took them out to the line in the summer. The best white sheets were put on the first line, the patched ones next and at the back went the underwear, blouses and socks. In a corner between two trees was a special line where Sister's nylons, handkerchiefs and white bibs from her habit hung to dry.

After lunch we would return to take the clothes off the line and the rest of the day would be spent helping Sister with the ironing. She put the folded sheets through a rotary iron and we had to work quickly to take them out and fold them again in perfect shape. They were then put into a basket and lifted upstairs and placed neatly into the hot press ready for use. The rest of the ironing like blouses and nightdresses was done in the dining room on a Saturday afternoon by another two girls. Two big heaving irons were used, one would be heating up in the Aga while the other was being used and had to be lifted out using a thick padded cloth as it got very hot. I loved ironing so I was glad when it was my turn.

I was given the task of sewing lace onto the new dancing

uniforms. I had to sew this lace onto the collars and cuffs of eight black velvet jackets. I loved sewing and was good at it so this was a treat for me, even though I was afraid I would make a mistake. The lace had to be gathered evenly without puckering which was very difficult with such a fine fine fabric. The Matron kept me out of school in the afternoons to do this. I was slow in the beginning because my stitches had to be invisible and I had to sit by the window as the light faded; the nuns rarely put the lights on. I never got a thank you for doing this work or told I was good, but I remember feeling that I was better than the others because I was asked and not them.

I also had the job of sewing Sister's stockings once a week. She would bring her bag to me while I was doing my homework. I loved this attention as it set me apart from the others. The bag was made from floral cotton fabric and had a drawstring on top. In this bag was a pair of scissors, needles and thread. I felt it was mine, as I was the only one who touched it. I would sew the ladders in the stockings and took great pride in doing a neat job. I took my time and every stitch was the same size. If it wasn't I would rip it down and do it again. I had a deep feeling of affection for Sister, I never showed it and my feeling was mixed with a fear of her. Still I enjoyed doing this job for her and felt proud. Again it was me who was asked, not anyone else.

At that time all I wanted to be when I grew up was a dressmaker. My best subjects at school were sewing, art and singing. Given a choice I would have given up school, which I hated as I always seemed to be lagging behind. I would have preferred to work in the home all day, but I was too young and the choice wasn't mine.

I was also on the school dancing team Irish dancing was encouraged in the school, in fact we had no choice in the matter. Fortunately I enjoyed it right up to the time I left. A lay teacher came in to the home for our hour-long lessons once a week. She was big and fat and didn't really teach us much. She would sit down and call out the routine of the dance and then it was up to us to perfect it. She rarely danced herself. When we went to Feis Maitiu we watched carefully how the others did their routines and how they all turned together and managed to be so light on their toes. I was very keen and coming up to the feiseanna I would hold classes in the evenings and we would perfect our performances.

We won several cups and medals and the nuns managed to give us some praise and I don't remember clearly but I expect we may have been given some sweets to celebrate. Another treat for winning the cup was going to the Cork Examiner office to have our photographs taken. We stood outside in our costumes holding the cup. Our return journey on the train was unusually unrestrained. The Matron was with us and did nothing to curb our excitement and even allowed us to shout out the windows of the train that we had won the cup.

CHAPTER 9

†††

Matron's Skivvies

The matron slept next door to my dormitory and one of the older girls shared her room, that one of the least-favourite jobs. If she was ever missing Matron would wake me up and call me into her. She would sit on a bentwood chair in her long floral flanelette nightie with buttons up the front. She would push the nightie back over her shoulders and, standing behind her, I would have to put my hand down her back and rub Deep Heat into it. She would direct my hand left and right, up and down and it always seemed like a long time before she said she had had enough. Then I would brush her long black hair, and had to stand while she said her prayers by the bed.

After that she got into bed and wrapped a black shawl around her shoulders. I would have to tuck her sheets and blankets in around her. The bed always seemed very high, as if it had two mattresses and she also had two dressing tables, one with a lovely swing mirror. On one of them sat a padded wicker-work basket in which she kept her pearls and brooches. On the other were her hairbrush and comb and a box of clips and a hairnet as well as her face creams. I remember looking in one of the drawers and seeing a large number of coloured nylon scarves which she wore when she went to Cork every Tuesday. In another drawer were her Pretty Polly nylons which were always returned to the package when they were washed.

As I left the room she would be having her milk and two Marietta biscuits. I was glad when these duties were done as I was always nervous that she would shout if I found a knot in her hair or did anything not quite to her liking. I was anxious to please her and keep on the right side of her and not give any reason for her to shout at me or pull my hair in temper.

My friend Marion had the job of cleaning Matron's room. She also had to attend to her every Saturday afternoon. Matron took over the washroom for about an hour and Marion would stand outside the door, running to fetch things from the bedroom. We never knew what Matron did for that hour, but she used a lot of cotton wool, boiling water and Pond's Cold Cream. She took a pride in her hands which always had pale pink varnish on her long nails and she had a bottle of Cutex. This was a problem for me to find when I stood in for Marion the first time. "Get me the Cutex", she roared and I had no idea what it was. I searched the room, but didn't know if I was looking for some form of soap or powder or cream. I was scared to ask her and was relieved to find the cuticle remover clearly marked on the label. It was in a drawer of one of her dressing tables. That was when I discovered all her personal belongings stored there.

After her hour's session in the bathroom the matron would go to her bedroom where Marion would have to set her hair. She used big hair rollers and setting lotion, but first she would have to go through her hair and pluck out each grey hair with a tweezers. This was an unpleasant process and every time a hair was pulled out the matron would give a yelp and dig Marion in the ribs. I managed to avoid this duty as Marion was always first choice and was called for any of Matron's errands. She also had to handwash all of Matron's clothes and I saw a box of Lux flakes in her room which was a big luxury. Apart from that, the whole business of Matron's laundry was kept a secret. We never saw the clothes drying and I still don't know where they were put. These duties took up a lot of Marion's time and it was strange that she never seemed to benefit in any way from this relationship with the matron. Matron didn't even appear to like her and never showed any appreciation of her help.

Also on Fridays Matron cut our nails and hair. She roughly cut our nails close to the quick and often drew blood. She also drew blood when she cut our hair as she often caught our ears or necks. She snipped roughly with the long black-handled scissors in short cuts. I always thought the back must be crooked, though

I couldn't see it. Anyone with big ears had their hair cut around their ears which showed them off even worse. She seemed to cut the hair of the better-looking girls even shorter than the others, and if it looked well she did her best to turn it into something unstylish. I wondered if I was good-looking as she often cut my hair and I always hated how I looked afterwards. I knew I had good skin and nice brown eyes as my Godmother often passed remarks saying that I was growing up to be a lovely girl. I took that to mean my looks rather than personality. As part of the Friday ritual we had to kneel up on a seat and show the heels of our socks. If there was a hole or a ladder, we got a belt of the side of the ruler on the heels and were told to darn them the next day.

Every day of our lives we had to fine-comb our hair. This was done with a nit-comb, a small black double-sided comb with close-set fine teeth. Our numbers were scraped onto them with a compass point and they were all kept in a small wooden box in a cupboard in what we called the Dressing Room. We all had to stand in a half-circle with the Matron watching us. We did our own first and then we did the smaller children's. The matron was never satisfied until she saw us going over to the waste-basket with a substantial handful of hair which we had dragged from digging deep into our scalps with the comb. Otherwise we weren't doing it properly. We made sure The matron saw us going to the basket.

If the matron saw anyone scratching their scalps she would check them. If any child had nits she had to wear a wool beret in bed. A strong- smelling lotion which could have been disinfectant was scrubbed into the hair and allowed to soak into the scalp. The beret was put on over the lotion and left on for two or three days, even at school. Everyone then knew you had nits. No-one else came to school in a beret like this. It was another way of separating us from the rest of the children at school.

The nuns in Rushbrooke primary school were extremely good to us. I remember feeling very relaxed with them. They never made us feel any different from the Outside Girls. We took part in the same activities as everyone else like Christmas plays, sports and the Sacred Heart Procession. There were also boys in the school. We were allowed to sit beside them and we mixed well with them. The only thing we were prevented from doing was joining the school band. I don't know why, perhaps because of the expense of an instrument.

Sixth class in that school was great fun as the head nun was often missing. We plucked up the courage to play some of the pranks that the Outside Girls used to do and we felt a great thrill when we weren't caught. It was just silly things like throwing the nun's gloves out the window onto the flat roof and watching one of the girls climb up to retrieve them before the nun got back. That made us feel normal. It was a horrible feeling coming in the back door of the orphanage after the freedom of the day at school. The darkness and quiet of the home compared with the laughter of school shook us back to reality very quickly.

We would study from four to six in the afternoons while at primary school. Saying The Angelus marked the end of that study time. Before returning to our homework after tea we would have to go into The Reck and dance around for half an hour. We waltzed with each other to the Gallowglass Ceili Band. We learnt the steps from the older girls and Matron would call out one - two- three, one-two-three, not often in time to the music, which confused us and we were always stepping on each others toes. "Use the whole room", she would shout, "don't forget the corner", "you're standing too close, arm's length only girls!". Sometimes Matron danced too and we would be afraid of being picked as her partner. She was a good dancer and always chose someone who could keep time to the music. She had big strides and it was difficult to keep up with her, so we often lost our footing and the only way to cope was to run and allow her to lift you along with her.

We were told this activity was to warm up The Reck for the younger children and Matron to watch television in, but I suspect it was also to warm ourselves up before we got back to our 'lessons'. The heating was kept so low all the time that we needed the warmth. I remember sitting in the study during the winter months with short sleeves, shivering with the the cold and rocking in the desk to keep warm.

We weren't allowed to talk to one another and even if we coughed we got a black look. If we needed to borrow something like a rubber or ruler we would dig someone with a pencil and make a sign for it. If the matron caught you she would make you stand out by the wall and then you couldn't finish your homework. On the way to school the next day you would have to copy someone else's work. When our copybooks were full we could get a new one from Matron. But not until every single line was full. Just one line left was enough for her to return it, so we often ended up borrowing pages from the Outside Girls. There was no point in borrowing from each other as the matron counted the pages in the copies.

We were given one pencil to last the year and shaved the end to put our names on. If we lost the pencil we would steal one from the Outside Girls and shave our own names onto it. It was a case of doing what was necessary. We were also issued with two hairgrips which we had to mind carefully, also one handkerchief (with our number on it) and in secondary school we got a pair of garters which had our names on. These were our only possessions and when the garters snapped we just tied a knot. By the end of the year the spring would be gone from the elastic and we had to tie them so tightly they made a deep mark in our legs. They didn't keep up the stockings very well, so we would walk along the road, constantly pulling them up.

Also to last the year we were given our Sunday dresses which were made for us by a dressmaker. They were usually made of cotton, patterned in three different colours, all in the same style which we were measured for by the dressmaker. We wore them every Sunday during the summer. As winter approached the winter clothes we changed into after school were taken out from one of the presses where they were folded with mothballs. The smell of camphor was very strong as we tried them on. Some of them were patched and we tried to avoid putting on these ones, but if they fitted, that was it - they were ours for the year. Our dark bottle-green pleated uniforms were also handed down from girls who left the orphanage. We would be given a large uniform which would be expected to last us as long as we went to school, which meant they were huge on us in first year and getting very small by sixth year . Occasionally we were given another in fifth or sixth year.

CHAPTER 10

†††

Becoming a woman

From the age of thirteen I used to cry a lot, mostly in bed. My body was changing and I was growing hair. I wanted to tell someone, as I thought there was something wrong with me. I thought only men grew hair on their faces and chests. I was afraid to tell anyone in case they told the matron and she would send me away because I was different from the other girls. I never saw the other girls' bodies. We used to dress in the morning by putting our hands inside our nightdresses. We would then remove the nightie when our clothes were on.

We changed our underwear on a Friday. We would kneel on the floor facing the wall with the Matron watching us. She watched to make sure we didn't look at each other. We had to line up and show the seat of our knickers to her. If they were soiled we had to wear them on our heads for everyone to see. The matron would call us Soilybags at every opportunity. If we had to wear the knickers on our heads we used to see our way around by looking out one of the legs and would have to wear them until we went to bed that night. I remember feeling very ashamed in front of the younger ones. When we got older we got clever and washed our knickers on a Thursday night and put them under the mattress to dry overnight. I remember going to school on Fridays with damp knickers. I didn't mind as it was better than having soiled ones for Matron.

Later when I graduated to Our Lady's dormitory from the Sacred Heart dormitory I used to peep at some of the girls getting dressed. Two or three of them had an extra garment. It was a shapeless piece of fabric with straps for the arms and lathes of string. It was supposed to keep them flat at the chest as they were very well developed. After a while I had to wear one of these bodices along with the other girls when we did Irish dancing on stage. The Matron tied them so tight we could hardly breathe.

When my breasts started to grow I used to pull my uniform straight. I didn't like the bumps they made in my uniform. Also I was afraid of wearing a bodice. Some of the Outside Girls had big breasts which stood out. I used to ask myself why mine were so small, yet I didn't want mine to show either. I tried to figure out why their mothers allowed them to come to school like that. I thought it was dirty to show your bumps.

I got my first period when I was thirteen and in sixth class in primary school. I went to the toilet and saw blood on my knickers. I told Chrissie, who was also an orphan, but older than me. I knew she knew what it was because she was one of the girls who used the small room for washing 'those things'. I knew something was to happen to me when I reached a certain age because the older girls washed something discreetly but I never knew just what. I used to peep into the red bucket when no-one was looking, to see what they were, but there was a terrible smell from the bucket. The towels were washed and put into the bucket until the end of the week when they would be boiled with washing soda and hung out in little bunches to dry on the line.

Chrissie told the teacher, and the teacher, who was a nun, asked me if I wanted to go home. I said I didn't. At about 5pm that evening while I was doing my homework, the matron called my name to come upstairs. I was afraid. I remember asking another girl what I should say. Matron asked me to show her my knickers. She slapped me across the face and called me an old woman. She told me not to tell the others. That must be how none of us found out about the others having their periods. She gave me a towel to put on. It was made of calico and was about the size of a baby's nappy. This had to be turned at opposite corners and a thick belt went through loops on the other corners tied in a big bow. We were given six towels and if you needed a seventh one you had to take someone else's. At 5pm each evening you changed your towel. You washed it out in cold water and carbolic soap. It could take up to an hour to get the stain out.

When I was in the last years at secondary school I got some money from a friend and would buy sanitary towels from the school machine. I would keep my calico towel folded in my bag until school finished and then put it on again before I went back. It was like putting on a piece of cardboard.

Our bed linen was changed every three weeks. One morning I woke up and my nightdress was full of blood from a heavy period. I was terrified; I told my friend Marion and we planned to get rid of it together. I was sixteen at the time. I put it into my schoolbag and we took a different route into school where no one could spot us. We tore up the nightdress and threw it over the wall by the railway station. I was very uneasy all day at school, I was sure someone would find it and bring it back to the home as my number was on it. We all had a number on our clothes, mine was number 6. For what seemed like months that nightdress was still visible in the briars over the wall. I kept hoping it would disintegrate or the wind or the rain would take it away. It did eventually seem to get smaller and smaller until one day was gone. Matron did of course notice it was missing from the laundry and accused me of getting rid of it in the hopes of getting a new one. I had to wear my second nightdress for weeks until a new long-sleeved flanelette one was made by the dressmaker for me. Matron never learned the full story about the nightdress.

We used the Washing Room for our daily wash. This room had twenty wash basins. We had to take our jumpers off and stand in our vest and knickers and wash our faces, hands, knees, necks and under our arms. I used to be shy about lifting up my arms because of the hairs. I was aware of the smell of body odour and didn't want anyone else to see the hairs, especially the matron. She used to tell us not to forget under the arms and I thought she only wanted to look and see who had hairs. I always washed quickly and dressed.

We had our weekly bath on Fridays before tea. Thirteen of us used the same water. If you were towards the end of the line the water was very cold and thick with grease. Up to the age of thirteen one of the older girls had to bathe you. Sometimes the older girl would only be a year older and I remember undressing for the bath and trying to hide myself. Some of the older girls were nice and used the bathtowel to hide you if you were shy. I felt very cross with the girls who looked at you in the bath or washed you, when they knew you could do it yourself.

Matron used to look into the bathroom to make sure you were being washed. Even when we were sixteen the matron still opened the bathroom door to see if we were washing ourselves properly. The matron said to me once that I was getting too big and would have to wear a bodice soon, but apart from for Irish dancing, I never got one.

A girl of nineteen stayed in the orphanage while she was attending the School of Commerce in Cork. When she left early for the train I used to look into her locker and examine her bra. I wondered what it would be like to wear one. I didn't believe my breasts would ever grow that big. They never did.

In the early sixties when we went for a day at the beach we had to tuck our dresses inside our knickers to paddle as we had no swimsuits. I was eleven or twelve at the time and I found it very embarrassing. The other people on the beach would be looking at us so we would try to hide behind each other. I always thought there was someone looking at me and would blush if anyone talked to me.

In the late sixties we got swimsuits. That was worse as now our bodies were on show for everyone to see. I used to walk hunched over to hide myself and I was also afraid that my pubic hair would peep through. In later years when I was in my twenties and thirties and had a good figure, I still never felt comfortable on the beach.

CHAPTER 11

†††

The Routine in Rushbrooke

On Saturday afternoons we learned to knit. We sat in benches around the room, in our own place according to our ages. If we dropped a needle we had to stay standing or the girl beside us was told to give us a smack, usually on the face. I was often smacked in the face by girls only months older or younger than me. I also had to do the same to them. I hated doing this, but you had to do as you were told. If you held back and tried not to hurt them, you would get a smack yourself. The Matron had to hear the sound of a good belt and after a while you didn't really care as long as long as it wasn't you getting it.

The floor was wooden and the sound of the needle dropping was loud, there was no denying what had happened. My stitches were so tight on the needle as a result that my hands got sweaty and the wool would hardly move on the needles.

When I think back on how I would hit other children I find it hard to believe I did it as I hated the violence so much, but we had to or else get a worse beating ourselves. I was often put in charge of one of the younger children's dormitories known as The Angels. I would have to stand at the door from half past six when they went to bed, until every one of them was asleep. Sometimes they would be a bit restless or crying and I would shout at them to stop or I would kill them. This usually worked without having to go further and smack them.

We all told tales on one another because if you told a tale on someone else, you would not get into trouble yourself. It was a way of looking after yourself, and this you did regardless of the punishment the other person got. There was no loyalty amongst us. If someone didn't own up, you told the Matron, that's the way it was. Often we were accused of doing something we hadn't and we would get a beating until we admitted to it. We often confessed when we hadn't done something, just to avoid a worse beating.

The only good thing about this recreation time was the fact that the radio would be on. This was where I learned a lot of old Irish songs which I still sing today. I used to practice in the toilet, we weren't allowed to sing in the home, there was no question of walking around singing or making unnecessary noise. Songs like The Old Rustic Bridge, Down the Old Bog Road, I Love You Because (Jim Reeves was a big favourite) were all hits at the time.

After we had done our knitting we were left to play in the room. The Matron used to sit by the oil fire and read or watch us. We used to comb one another's hair with our hands, fold the sleeves of each others jumpers, and fold the tops of our socks in different ways. It was something to do out of boredom. If Matron thought two girls were becoming good friends she would separate them. If we walked to school with the same girls for a few mornings, she would separate us.

The one real opportunity for being with a special friend was on a Saturday when we went to confession. Two priests came once a month to the church in Rushbrooke and we used to look out the window to see which priests were there. We dressed up for confession with a wool beret and a coat. We fussed as we got dressed, arranging our hair hoping that there would be boys in the church. There never were.

Most of us would sit at one side of the church waiting for our favourite priest and when the other looked out we would all move uneasily in the queue. Sometimes he asked if we had been to confession and rather than go into him we would say yes. We would then have to return later to have our sins heard. In all my years at school since my first Holy Communion I always confessed the same sins - *"Bless me Father for I have sinned, I told lies, I was disobedient and gave back answers".*

On Sundays after dinner at 2pm we used to go for a walk towards what was called The Grove. This was a wooded area and we were allowed to climb the trees and run around. We would make patterns on the ground with stones, each of us would have our own house etched on the ground and would sit in the middle pretending we owned it. We also got a great kick out of jumping over the cow pats.

On our way there and back Sister and the Matron walked behind us. Everyone knew we were the convent girls. Young boys would hide behind their garden walls and throw stones at us and call us Golliwogs. It was very hurtful, but even more hurtful was meeting our friends from school and not being allowed to stop to talk to them or call across the road to them. Matron would shout "Keep looking ahead!" and would march us on.

On other Sundays we stayed on the lawn to play. We had to keep running around, especially if someone visited the church. Matron would see the passer-by approaching and would clap her hands loudly and we knew that that meant we were to liven up and look happy. We were never allowed to sit on the grass or sit on the garden benches. If we wanted to rest we went into the church and pretended to pray. I loved chewing the hot soft candlegrease which I broke off the burning candles in front of the statue of St. Anthony. I always went to the top of the church to genuflect hoping that a nun would see me praying so devoutly.

At around half past five we would gather in rows kneeling on the grass to say the Rosary. This would be followed by various prayers appropriate to the month and always finished off with a prayer for past pupils and the Holy Souls. We were very conscious of our friends from the school passing by and seeing us having to spend our day like this. We tried to rush the prayers, but Matron would slow us down if she heard the pace quickening. Prayer punctuated our day; we went to mass every second day and said the Angelus at the table before supper and followed that by Grace before Meals.

I often felt faint at Mass and would sit up on the pew. If Matron saw me she would tell me to 'kneel up straight and stop looking for notice!'. Quite regularly I would end up on the floor having fainted and would be lifted up on to the pew with my head put between my legs. I would recover with the sound of Matron's voice telling me to 'kneel up again Drennan!' One morning I went to the altar to receive Holy Communion and felt faint. I must have swayed to the side because the priest missed my mouth and the Host dropped onto the floor. It was a shocking moment. All the nuns could see me as they were sitting at the side of the alter with full view. The priest bent down and picked up the Bread and put it onto the paten, but I was in disgrace. I recovered from my faint very quickly and prepared myself for the backlash.

"Where is she? Where is she? She has disgraced us all! Imagine dropping the Blessed Sacrament on the floor!" Sister caught me by the hair and pulled me along the hallway of the home and made me kneel there until the others had finished their breakfast in the dining room. I remember feeling worse about the fact that I was responsible for putting her into a bad mood for the day, which would affect all the other children. Even Sister Ita looked cross with me and I found it hard to look at her or any of my friends in the face. Sister reminded me of it for a few days afterwards shouting "Get out of My Way!" which did little to help my nervousness when I went to the altar again.

All of this did little to put me off Sunday mass as I was in the choir. This meant that I had to go to mass a second time and dodge my chores. Only a few of us were picked for the choir which made me feel good. I enjoyed singing and loved the Latin hymns which were so beautiful. Father O'Connor had a powerful voice which blended well with the girls voices and he would look over to us encouragingly while we were singing. The nuns never sang.

Once a year we had a special treat. We called it Fitzpatrick's Tour as it was sponsored by a Mr. Fitzpatrick who lived near the home. We never met him but he paid for these wonderful trips. One of these trips was a day spent on a liner anchored off Cobh. There was great excitement. We were never told by Sister where we were going, so the wonder of it all was great. We had the day off school for the treat and I remember the excitement as we put on our best dresses. A big bus came and took us down to the harbour; from there we went by tug to the liner. I remember looking at this big huge ship with delight as we approached it. We spent the day on the liner, playing on swings and slides and we had a party with lemonade, sweets and lots of cakes. After the day we came home exhausted. It was the best day of the year. Another good one was the Dockyard Party which was held at Christmas. This was for the orphanage and paid for by the dockyard who gave us presents as well. Two black men used to be Santa's helpers and they used to show us Laurel & Hardy films. They also threw sweets and wrapped biscuits in the air for us to catch. We tried to get as many as we could and stuffed ourselves with them.in case they would be taken from us later.

Another treat was during the summer when we were taken by bus to various beaches like Garryvoe and Youghal. During these outings we were noticeable as we stayed together and carried a suitcase full of sandwiches. The wasps would be attracted to our jam sandwiches so I never really enjoyed them. It wasn't all fun. One of the days I accidentally hit someone on the eye with a stone aimed at the water and she ended up with three stitches. I was punished severely by not getting pocket money that day. This pocket money was usually about six old pence. This would buy us a packet of Silvermints for Sister and an ice-cream for ourselves. If Sister wanted an ice-cream it was usually a melted blob by the time we got back to her. We might as well have licked it on the way back, but we didn't dare. In later years the nuns were allowed to wear swimsuits. We were always hoping to see them in one but they would hide in the sand dunes to sunbathe. If Sister went into the water to swim we would have to get out.

The most daring thrill for us during the summer was when we would sneak off from the garden to the beach at Whitepoint where we always hoped we would see boys. Nothing ever happened as it was so obvious who we were that they ignored us. Still, we got a thrill out of escaping and getting back without anyone knowing. We never got caught, the younger ones were well threatened by us not to tell.

At Christmas we were given the opportunity to sing and dance in the Christmas pantomime which was held in the YMCA hall in Cobh. A new priest, Fr. O'Connor, arrived and took a huge interest in the children in the home and persuaded Sister to allow us to perform. When I was ten or eleven I was chosen along with seven others to be a fairy in Cinderella.

The dressmaker made beautiful lacy dresses; mine was yellow. We had to sing and dance and we rehearsed in the home with Fr. O'Connor. For the two weeks of the show we would take a nap in the afternoons and Sister would give us a few sweets. We would be collected by car and brought to the hall and thick make-up put on our faces. Thick sticks of oily red lipstick were used and we loved the big blob of rouge on our cheeks which was very difficult to get off afterwards.

The Matron would constantly give us directions from the wings and we spent more time listening to her than concentrating on what we were doing. I'm sure the audience could hear her and we were scared to make a mistake. During another concert one night we were supposed to dance a reel in our stockinged feet. I forgot to take off my big brown shoes and the Matron called at me from the wings to take them off immediately. Fr. O'Connor shouted from the lighting platform to leave them on so I danced around in complete confusion. Matron persisted so somehow I managed to kick them off into the wings and continued without them. I got a terrible doing off when the dance was finished. Despite this I enjoyed the whole business of getting out on stage in front of people and it was the best part of Christmas in those years.

Those of us who didn't receive pocket money from their

families for Christmas were given some by Sister. We all went to Cork by train to do our shopping with it. We got enough money for the train fare and presents for the Sister, Matron and Cook. If we ran out of money by the time we got to the cook's present, two of us would club together and buy something between us. We usually got soap or a handkerchief for Sister, and talc or soap for Matron. Writing paper was cook's favourite present. We had to account to the Matron for every penny spent which was not too difficult. We wrapped the presents and left them on Sister's telephone table and Matron's were left on the breakfast table. I enjoyed giving Cook her present as she appreciated it so much and thanked us. The other two didn't. Those presents we gave to Sister and Matron were later used as prizes in our annual whist drive.

For breakfast on Christmas Day we had grapefruit, followed by a slice of ham, bread and marmalade (this was special and to this day I still have the same treat). We had the usual dinner of turkey, roast potatoes and vegetables followed by Christmas Pudding. After dinner the table was cleared and laid for the Christmas supper. Plastic tablecloths with Christmas motifs were used and little basket-shaped doilies held portions of sweets. Tiny sandwiches of chicken and ham spread were arranged on individual plates with a couple of fairy cakes on each. We all got a cracker and a party hat. Everything was left in place until the Bishop, priests and nuns from the parish had viewed this sumptuous spread. When they left, some of the fairy cakes were removed and the fruit cake in the centre of the table taken away for use over the coming weeks. Some of the sweets were also removed.

We were allowed to pull the crackers when Matron told us to and we ate whatever goodies were left on the table. We had plenty to eat, but never so much to allow us to over-indulge. After we had done the washing up we went down to the recreation room where we sat around and waited for Sister to come. One of the older girls was given the job of removing the presents hanging on the tree. As each name was called out, we came forward and the others clapped as we received our gift. This was usually a Christmas stocking when we were seven or under, or soap and toothpaste for the under fifteens. Over fifteens received nylons, nightdresses or shoes so they would have a decent pair when they left the home.

These presents were left on the benches around the room for the week for the visitors to view. By the time we were allowed to have them a week later we had lost our enthusiasm for them. When the gift of soap ran out it was back to the usual carbolic for the rest of the year. The toothpaste was also replaced by the carbolic soap when it ran out, so we used to squeeze every last bit out of the tube. There were no keys on our lockers in the washroom so sometimes we swapped tubes with someone who had a fuller one.

CHAPTER 12

†††

The Cook

Sister Ita, the cook, was lovely. She was one of two nuns in the home and for all the years I was there I was very fond of her. She was very warm and always smiling, but as I grew older I realised that she was as frightened as we were of Sister and of the woman we called Matron.

Sister Ita was responsible for all the meals in the home, though we helped her from time to time. On Sunday mornings after mass the bread for the week would be buttered. There was a big machine for cutting the loaves of bread. They would go into it three at a time and a rotary blade would slice them thinly and Sister would catch the batches of slices as they came out of the machine. We were not allowed to go near it. We would mix a pound of butter with a pound of margarine and two of us would sit on one side of a big green Formica-topped table and work through the slices, piling them into shape and then placing them in two deep bins, separating each loaf with butter wrapper. The heels of the loaves were kept together and were dried out in the oven for the secondary school girls to have with hot milk after school. We all used to make a dive for the smallest pieces as they were so horrible.

The meals were predictable. Breakfast consisted of Cornflakes on a Monday, a boiled egg on Sunday, and porridge the rest of the week. A large plate of bread would be placed in the middle of the table and it had to finished off between the four or five of us, whether we were hungry or not. Two girls went around with large teapots serving tea which was already milked and sugared. This tasted quite well except on Sundays when there was a distinct taste of Silvo from the pot which was cleaned on Saturdays. We took turns to get up to make breakfast. When it was our week we got up with Sister at 6.30 am and had to wait around while Sister poked at the Aga to get it to heat up. We put the kettles to boil and the porridge which had been soaking overnight to cook in its big pot. We stood around trying to get warm in the cold dark kitchen while Sister went next door into the convent. Before she went she would swallow a cup of hot salted water. I don't know why. Perhaps it prevented her from becoming ill, as I don't even remember her missing a day of duties.

Dinner consisted of Stew on Mondays with soup first which had been made from Sundays leftovers. We all had to break up our bread and put it into the soup. It was a meal in itself. We got fish (smoked haddock) on Fridays and a slice of meat with vegetables on the other days. I hated the gravy which always had lumps of fried onion in it. We had that same brown gravy every day and Matron poured the gravy all over everything on the plate.

We would have to take second helpings, usually of potatoes, if there were any left over. We would have to rush our food as we only had three quarters of an hour before the taxi would come to take us back to school. This sometimes caused the younger children to vomit which made Matron very angry. She would shout at them and force them to eat their vomit until they kept it down. This would make the rest of us feel ill, but we got used to it. We learned to deal with extra helpings by hiding them in our aprons when Matron wasn't looking and putting them later into the dog's dish in the kitchen. Sister Ita would see the dog's dinner multiplying and would pass comment, but never within the hearing of the matron.

Our lunch main course was followed by Rice Pudding or Sago with a blob of jam in the middle. Jelly and custard or apple tart and cream were Sunday treats and Sister Ita's apple tart was superb. For supper we got bread which was always brown soda on a Friday, with cheese, on the other weekdays we got white bread with a slice of black pudding or a sausage. On Saturday we got Shepherd's Pie and on Sunday a slice of fruit brack. This would be accompanied by tea on Sunday and cocoa the rest of the week. We learned to drink the cocoa while it was hot and before a skin would form. If a skin did form we would have eat it as we were not allowed to leave anything inside our cup.

There was a lot of nagging done at the dining table. The older girls taught the younger ones how to eat silently and if a spoon or fork was dropped they would be given a clatter. Soup was never slurped, crumbs were never dropped (if they were, they had to picked up and eaten) and we were not allowed to speak while eating. When Matron decided that everyone was finished and all the plates had been gathered up, she would ring a little brass bell and announce "**You may talk now**". Everyone would be afraid to be the first to talk so there would be a low mutter and Matron would repeat herself "**You may talk now!**". We knew if we didn't speak up and talk that this ten-minute privilege would be taken away from us. This happened a few times and the bell was rung again and we were told to leave the room in silence and get on with the washing up.

We had our different chores after supper: one girl would wash up in a stainless bowl using boiling water and soap which was enclosed in a plastic container like a sieve. When you shook it in the water it would make bubbles like washing up liquid does. Two of us had to dry up, sometime with teatowels which were already wet, and when the delph was dry it would be passed through a hatch into the dining room where three more girls set the tables for breakfast.

All the goodies were kept in the pantry. Things like cakes, sugar, apples, cooked meats, jellies and cheese. Sometimes I used to steal a half pound of cheese before going to bed. I loved cheese, but found the half pound a bit too much. I had to eat it though: I couldn't share it as someone would tell, and I couldn't return some of it as it would be more noticeable. I choked the last pieces down and then hid the wrapping until the morning when I hid it in my knickers and dumped it at school. Sister Ita never seemed to notice the cheese was missing. There were other treats kept in the pantry which had been cooked during cookery classes which were held on Saturday afternoons.

A Mrs. Kenefick came from Cork to teach us how to make Queen cakes, sponges, semolina, fish pies, Queen of Puddings and other treats. She taught us how to scramble eggs and this dish, and most of the others would end up as Matron's supper. Mrs Kenefick was quite strict but fair and she was encouraging and interested in us. We enjoyed her classes. There was something about her, she called us by our first names, which was unusual (we were always shouted at by our surname or full name by Matron). Mrs. Kenefick seemed to enjoy teaching us and was like a kind aunt to us all. She also taught us how to iron properly, remove stains and starch clothes. I learned a lot from her and still iron my shirts the way she taught me.

When we were finished our cookery class Sister Ita would come in to see what we had cooked. She would admire our work and taste it. We had to leave all the food on the table and she would store it for visitors or Matron's afternoon tea.

We would tell Sister Ita when it was our birthday and she would pass in a fairy cake through the hatch from the kitchen to the dining room. If the Matron felt like it or had some excuse to punish you, she would take the cake and give it to someone else on your table. This was very hurtful. You felt bad because Sister Ita had gone to the trouble of giving you a treat, and also it was the only recognition of your birthday from the nuns, and it had been taken away. We never sang Happy Birthday or received any gifts, apart from some home-made cards which we gave each other.

Sister Ita would give us the mixing bowl to lick and if the Matron caught us Sister Ita would say we were helping with the washing up. Matron would then catch us by the hair and throw us out of the kitchen. I often wondered if she was trying to punish us or Sister Ita who was obviously scared of Matron. You could feel her tensing up when she came into the kitchen; her face would go red and quickly she would find something to do rather than stand and talk to her.

Matron used wooden spoons a lot to beat the children with. The cook never complained directly to Matron about the broken spoons, but you could hear her shouting in the kitchen complaining that she had no decent wooden spoons left in the kitchen for mixing her cakes. It was her only way of getting her point across. Sometimes there were no wooden spoons left in the kitchen drawer and we would be sent around the house collecting them. It was easy to find them as we just had to go to where the last person got a beating.

Many years later when I returned to visit the home I would bring small gifts for Sister Ita. She would be delighted with any small gesture and when we asked what she would like she always wanted birthday and Christmas cards as she had no money to buy them herself. She had come from a poor family and had only a few relatives who rarely visited her.

When anyone got a birthday card by post they kept it and used it again and sent it to someone else. As we never had money to buy cards, we would cut out the writing or stick a patch over it and rewrite the cards. This was great fun, it was a way of giving a gift to a friend. One of my friends who lived in the town (she was known as an Outside Girl, we were known to them as Convent Girls) used to save her family's cards and give them to me. As I got older if we found some paper I would save it for making greeting cards later.

One year Sister saw what I was doing and she gave me more paper to make a batch which she said were to be sold for charity. I also made St Patrick's Day badges. I used cardboard, tinfoil, sequins, thread and tiny beads and these too were sold at the school for charity. I loved making these cards and still make my own for the family. On our Sunday walks I would collect matchboxes thrown in the gutter and the silver foil from cigarette packs which I made into book marks and the matchboxes I converted into beds for paper dolls. I made bird boxes from iced lolly sticks and hoped that birds would nest in them. I tried for years but never succeeded in attracting them.

I wasn't always in favour with my favourite nun either. I remember the time I knocked her veil off when we were playing ball on one of our summer outings. When it happened it was a major disaster. She was as embarrassed as if she had been stripped naked. My punishment was to sit down on the grass for the rest of the day. I really felt bad about it as I liked Sister Ita and I felt I had upset her. It was an accident, but I still felt terribly guilty. In later years I was happy I could bring some pleasure to her. When the nun's habits were redesigned to allow hair to be revealed, I would bring back some Grecian 2000 to Sister Ita so she could dye her hair. She was delighted with this, though it would have been thought of as vanity. She is still alive today and retired in the convent in Rushbrooke.

CHAPTER 13

†††

Violence in the Home

Sister often used a black strap for beating the children. It was thick and stiff and was probably made of leather. It was about two and a half feet long and kept in Sister's Press in the hall. This was a tall cupboard with a strange hospital-like smell and though we were never allowed to see into it we had a good idea that it contained things like sticking plaster, medicines, iodine, writing paper, a pair of scissors, files and a small box of sweets. I still have the scar on my left thumb when Sister held my arm behind my back and used the scissors to cut off my wart. She also gave me a sweet from the cupboard that day to stop me crying. If any of the children were sick or needed a bandage it was at The Press they were attended to. If Sister remembered your birthday and if you were one of her pets she called for you to meet her at The Press. Only on that day could you be sure that it was a treat that was going to be given from The Press. One sweet, usually a boiled one, was the treat and we relished it and it made our day. Unless someone else spoiled it for you.

The black strap was taken from The Press for serious offences like being kept in school for not having a book. The reason for not having this book was often because someone else was using it. I had to share with four others from the home and some days it was someone else's turn to use it in another classroom. Though the nuns at the school knew this, we still were punished and not allowed to share with the person next to us and were put outside the door and told to stay in after school to catch up.

One day the whole class was kept in late. One of the Outside Girls put drawing pins on the teacher's chair. The teacher was the only male teacher and we had to call him Professor. He walked around the classroom with the pins stuck in his trousers and the class was in stitches laughing. No-one would tell him why we were laughing and we all got detention. When we arrived back at the home Sister had already been informed of what had happened. The rest of the children were rounded up to witness our shame and to see us being used as examples. We stretched across the table in the dressing room upstairs and our knickers were pulled down. This was particularly embarrassing for me as I had my period at the time and I knew everyone could see my sanitary towel. The black strap was brought out and the five of us got about ten lashes each. They were long stinging stokes and tightening your muscles didn't help, nor did putting your hand there as it got a lash too and could be even worse. One of the others threatened to tell her mother and she was silenced with another lashing.

Another time I got the Black Strap was when I was cleaning a window. It was a big sashed window on the first floor. I said to the other girl that I was going to sit out on the window-sill for fun. I was sitting on the sill facing inwards with the window resting on my lap when the nun came around the corner and looked in the door which faced the window. She got such a fright she dropped the bowl of water she was carrying and shouted at me to get in immediately. She accused me of looking for attention from the men working in the garden, though there were no men there that day, and went downstairs for the Black Strap. I was also put standing outside the dining room door during suppertime. I got nothing to eat for that meal.

Another time in the same room I jumped from a ladder onto a bed. The ladder was there to allow us to dust the open rafters high up in the ceiling. The ladder fell towards the picture of the Holy Flower and broke the glass. Once again the strap was produced. Three years ago when I visited the home I noticed that picture on the same wall. I told the sister in charge my story and she offered the picture to me as a memento. I hadn't the heart to refuse it.

I don't remember why and I often wonder if it was out of the matron's frustrations that we were punished in various ways. The

Matron would often pinch our faces. She would clench her teeth and cry out "Come over here, you Drennan!" A rush of thoughts would come into my head as I started to shake with fear. Who had told tales on me, and what had I done and which punishment was I going to get this time. With her hand forming into a claw she would stretch out her arm and either drag you hair or else she would place her thumbs in our mouths and dig her long sharp nails into our cheeks. This caused an intense sting as the nails pierced both inside and outside our cheeks. The imprints were so deep they would have to be covered with Calomine lotion before going to school. My mother came once when I had these prints on my face and Sister told her that the cat had scratched me. I couldn't say anything.

Another time my friend Marion got a My Weekly from one of the Outside Girls at school. When she was finished reading it she gave it to me. The Matron found it in my bag (she regularly checked our schoolbags) and confronted me with it. She wanted to know if I had brought this terrible magazine into the home, shouting at me that I had a yellow streak in me. I took this to mean that I was a bad child, though later I wondered if it referred to the fact that my father could have been foreign. When I said I hadn't brought the magazine into the home she demanded to know who had given it to me. I wouldn't tell on my friend (by the age of sixteen we had become loyal to each other) and she beat me on the top of my head as I knelt on the floor. She was wearing Dr. Scholl wooden sandals and this is what she used as her weapon. I begged her to stop as I felt I was going to faint and it was only when one of the older girls came in and shouted at her that she stopped.

Usually bedwetting was one of the reasons for punishment, as was a bad report from school. There was no apparent upper or lower age limit for punishment. I remember a friend who was probably just seven years old being sent into the coal shed for a full day. This is where the cats were put at night and this little girl was afraid of cats. Her supper and her breakfast next morning were brought to her there. Of course her bedwetting wasn't cured for as long as I remember. I recall that when she was about ten the dressmaker made knickers of mackintosh which she had to wear to school as punishment (she never wet her pants at school) and she creaked as she walked and her uniform stuck out as they were bulky.

Three or four girls who were frequently sick at the table had their vomit fed back to them until they kept it down. The reason they probably got sick in the first place was that they were forced to have second helpings of dinner rather than waste it. One of these girls was always sickly. She died of Leukaemia at the age of fifteen.

Some girls bit their nails. To cure us of this habit, sheets of newspaper would be wrapped from just below the wrist to above the elbow and tied with twine so we couldn't bend our elbows. This was also done to children who had chicken pox or measles to stop them from scratching. It worked, as it was impossible to bend your arm and get it anywhere near your face. It still didn't cure me of biting my nails, which I still do to this day.

The nuns owned the farm at the back of the home and it was worked by two old farmers. One time, as punishment for tearing books, three children afraid of pigs were sent one at a time to an enclosed pigsty to stand with the three fat sows. They were dressed in long raincoats and wellingtons and left there overnight. We could hear their screams all night.

What seemed the worst punishment of all was for the same 'offense' when the girls were forced to crawl along the floor. With their jumpers and vests pulled back to expose their bare skin we had to line up in two rows and beat them as they filed past us a few times. They sobbed as they crawled past us, afraid to cry out too loudly for fear of longer punishment. We were all about twelve or thirteen at this stage and growing loyal to each other and it was horrible having to do this to our friends and face them afterwards. About three months later a helper (an ex convent girl) in the kitchen admitted to tearing the books which the girls had been punished for. We knew all along it couldn't have been the young girls as the number pages which had been torn at once would have needed an adults strength to do it. There was never an apology from the Matron who had beaten a confession out of them.

One Saturday morning I couldn't take any more of the matron's shouting, the children crying and repeating I'm sorry, I'm sorry I'm sorry. The sounds built up in my head and I felt I was going to burst. I was polishing the dormitory floor and felt I had to escape and tell someone outside the home what was going on. I went downstairs and told the cook about what was happening upstairs and she told me to tell Sister, I didn't want to so I ran out the house and out to the road. I was adamant I would never go back inside. I hesitated for a few seconds as I didn't know where to go and who to tell. I then realised that no-one would believe me and that I really had no friends outside. I also realised that I had broken a major rule of going outside the gate and a fear crept over me.

What would happen me if I got caught and who would stand up for me? Would I be sent to the Good Shepherds as was so often threatened? I didn't know who they were, but we knew that it was where naughty girls were sent. Quickly I decided to go back into the back yard where I stayed crying for a while. Sister saw me and knocked on her office window and beckoned me in. When I refused she came out and asked me what was wrong. I told her that Matron was beating one of the girls upstairs and that I couldn't stand it any longer. She quietly told me to dry my eyes and go back to my duties and I was surprised at both her kindness and at my own courage in telling what happened. I was even more surprised that Matron never retaliated. Perhaps Sister never said anything to her. It was hard to judge Sister's reaction to anything. She was inclined to be moody and these moods affected the atmosphere in the home.

It could be tense when every sound seemed to be magnified and it would only be a matter of time before one of us would get a belt from Sister or Matron who was also affected by Sister's moods. At these times it was wise to keep out of their way even if it meant holding back going to the toilet. She spent a lot of time in the convent at the other side of the church and I often wondered what went on there to affect her moods. I would watch her face as she came through the study door and I could tell what was going to come next by her expression. When her face was red this was a bad sign and time to go under cover. The only time I remember Sister being in good form was when Miss Bullen came to visit and when we went to the beach, but we were never sure when the good mood would end, so we were never totally relaxed in her company.

I remember when Sister went to hospital for an operation. I was very worried that if she died the matron would be in charge. For the two weeks of her absence the matron was worse than ever. She continuously shouted and picked on those who were the nun's favourites, including me. I cried for the two weeks she was in hospital and even when the Matron asked me to say a decade of the Rosary I couldn't stop. I was greatly relieved when she came back to the home and things returned to normal.

CHAPTER 14

†††

The Change from Primary to Secondary School

Our years in Primary School were good. It wasn't until secondary school that we were to fully realise that as convent girls we were different from the rest. The nuns in secondary school called us Convent Girls and the name stuck with the students as well. The nuns didn't dislike all of us. They had their favourites who were bright and showed up the rest of us. We were the trouble-makers.

The five of us orphans in first year were given special notebooks which the nuns used for putting remarks in about our conduct or our homework. The matron would check the notebooks every day and if there was any remark that suggested we hadn't behaved, this was justification for a beating. "You're useless, you'll never be any good! You'll be just like your mother, you'll never get on!" she shouted if the remarks were unfavourable. I wonder if she ever thought that this constant reminder that I was worthless would affect me so much in later years. She said is so often I believed it myself.

When we went into first year in secondary school we were given the shoes of the girls who had just left sixth year. If they were too big we stuffed them with newspaper and tied string around them. This was not as bad as it sounded as we all had to change our shoes indoors to black 'rubber dollies'. Everyone else's were brown, but at least they were our own. We wore these shoes for PE, but I hated sports. This was mainly because I was ashamed of the stockings and garters we had to wear. At that stage tights had come into fashion and the Outside Girls all wore them. We still had to wear heavy stockings and garters and long knickers. We used to hide in the toilets rather than wear shorts which would show the mark of the garters on our legs. The head nun would catch us and send us back to PE. During my last year at school a few of us bought a few pairs of tights between us. We shared these on PE days and put them on before we got to school. We would leave our stockings in a carrier bag hidden in the bushes of the orphanage grounds and then change back into them on our return. One day the bag was missing when we got back. Someone had found it and handed it into the Matron. She was waiting for us when we got back and those who were wearing tights were giving a bad thrashing. Even worse punishment was the matron deciding to accompany us to school every day from then on. This meant we could no longer join our friends on the road and took the fun out of the journey.

I was often sent outside the classroom door for not knowing something. The head teacher would ask why you were outside the class and slapped you on the knuckles with the side of the ruler. She would send you back into the classroom crying as an example to the others. I didn't cry from the slap but from the disgrace of being outside the door. I felt different from the Outside Girls (the nuns called them *The Townspeople*); I felt I had no business being with them. If we changed classes I would wait until they had chosen their desks and then sit in whatever place remained. When we were told to bring a pound of meat for a cookery class we were given half a pound. If we need butter we got margarine, three eggs we got two. Everyone else brought their soup or stew home in a nice casserole dish. We would have a tin can. They were different from us. They had their own pencils and books and nice bits and pieces like fancy pencil cases and jewellry. They also had pocket money to spend on crisps, and hot soup and drinking chocolate from a machine in the school. The smell used to make me very hungry and I envied those girls. The secondary school overlooked the harbour. I spent hours looking out the window at the ships and boats coming and going. I watched the weddings and funeral parties as they came out of the church and wondered if that was ever going to be me in a white dress getting married.

I loved the sound of the bells of the Cathedral which rang out every hour and the sounds of the speedboats whizzing around the harbour. In my last year in secondary school those of us who were not taking science subjects learned to type. Most days we would be left on our own with pages to type.

On sunny days a couple of us would sneak out and hang around the town. The trick was to get from the gate to the road without being caught by a teacher looking out the window. In town, even though there was nothing to do, we enjoyed the freedom of walking around amongst the ordinary people and not having to walk in line. We were always afraid that someone would report us, though in our last year of school we didn't care too much. We never got caught and even if we had we would have back-answered Matron who was beginning to lose control of us. We were becoming braver and I think she got a bit softer.

Our lives were lightened every summer when the painters came to redecorate the orphanage. The Lenihan brothers did this work and we were always trying to distract them. If we passed under the ladder, they would shout down 'hello', and we were half afraid to answer back in case the matron heard us. We would find an excuse to go into the room where they were working just to speak to them and get noticed by them. They were very good-looking men in their twenties but they never took advantage of the situation. When we heard they were coming there was great excitement, everyone combed their hair and brushed their eyebrows and tightened the belts of their dresses to make them shorter and come above the knee.

Helen, one of the older girls was in charge of making the painters their afternoon tea. Helen was crazy about Donal, the youngest painter. She was coming down the stairs with the tray when she tripped and broke all the china cups which were used for our visitors. We could hear Sister shouting at her throughout the house. Helen was one of the girls who remembers having her ears pulled, she says that's why her ears stick out so much today.

Homework in the orphanage was done from 5 to 8.30 pm, taking a break for supper and the washing up. Between 7 and

8.30 the matron sat next door watching television. Between the two rooms there was a frosted glass window which we had to crawl under if we wanted to use the toilet. The matron did not allow us to leave the room for any reason. One evening the matron came out and saw Patsy, who used to sit next to me, crawling on the floor towards the door making her way to the toilet. Matron snapped 'What are you doing?" and I said I had dropped my pencil and that I had asked Patsy to look for it. She pulled my hair as punishment for dropping my pencil and expecting someone else to do my picking up for me.

CHAPTER 15
†††
Holidays

In all the years I spent in Cobh orphanage there were only two times when my mother took me on holiday. The first time was when I must have been about seven. My memory of it is vague, except that I ran around the hostel where Miss Bullen lived and my mother wouldn't allow me to see her undress. She made me face the wall while she changed into her nightdress and I remember being frightened of her and hiding under the bedcovers.

The next holiday I remember when I was eleven. She had written to say that she had got married. She had included a black and white photograph of the wedding day in which.she and Jim stood with his brother and sister outside a registry office. They looked quite happy and Jim looked like a nice person and I liked the idea of having a father. This my mother said was the reason she had married him - to give me a father. And I believed it and thought she would immediately take me away from the home to live with them. They both came in a taxi to take me away on a weeks holiday.

I had a borrowed a red tartan suitcase which had a zip around it and in it I had my change of clothes to last the week. They didn't get out of the taxi and I rushed into it and sat in the back seat with my mother. Jim turned around and introduced himself in a friendly way and I was thrilled. He seemed really nice. My mother was in good form and everything seemed wonderful. The taxi took us to the Woburn Guest House opposite Kent railway station in Cork. I was shown to my room at the opposite end of a long corridor to my mother and new father. I put the suitcase on the floor; there was nothing worth unpacking, just my nightdress, one pair of clean knickers and my toilet bag. They had told me to meet them downstairs in the bar so when I went down they were there already drinking and chatting to the landlord.

The whole week seemed like one long pubcrawl. My mother seemed to know someone in every pub and she would introduce Jim to them, but I was always left in a dark corner with a bottle of red lemonade and endless packets of crisps. There always seemed to be old men near me, all smoking and smiling. I don't remember any chat with Jim, he seemed to follow my mother around and did whatever she wanted. He was easy-going and I felt comfortable enough with him. Though I was bored I was afraid to move from where I was told to sit and passed the week looking forward to getting back to the home. I did have two days break from this routine when I was brought to a house in Churchfield on the northside of Cork.

I stayed with a Mrs Walsh who had two daughters of my age. I enjoyed their company though they were very wild. They would climb out the windows at night to go to dances nearby, but I was too afraid to go with them. During these two days my mother brought me with her to St. Finbarrs Hospital where I met a woman and her twenty-four year old blind daughter. This woman wanted to adopt me and bring me to England to be a companion for her daughter. She said I would have lovely dresses and would live in a big house and would have whatever I wanted. This seemed like the best thing that ever happened to me. I was delighted with the offer and started to picture myself in lovely new clothes.

For the week I had little other conversation with my mother except when I talked about not doing my Inter cert. She said she thought it was better for me to finish my education in the home and then she would take me to London where she was living with Jim. I was a bit confused at this as I thought she had forgotten about the adoption. I was too nervous to question it and went back to the home in a muddle about my future. From the way my mother and Jim dressed I was under the impression that they had loads of money and I was expecting to go back to the home with some new clothes or bits and pieces. They bought nothing for me. A few months later Sister told me that my mother wouldn't sign the adoption papers to go to the woman in London. She didn't say why.

After that, communication with my mother was just occasional. I received Christmas cards and if there was ever anything in them like money I never received it. The letters were opened before we got them and she said afterwards she had sent a few pounds each Christmas. In my last year in secondary school (5th year) I sent letters to my mother through one of the Outside Girls who would post them to her. In return I would receive the odd pound which I would share with my four schoolfriends. We would buy crisps and soup from the machine in school and paid for the tights we wore for PE. We felt very normal being able to do this and the nun never found out.

My mother wrote more often in my last year at the home. I would beg her to take me away because I was really tired of all the nagging from Sister and Matron and I wanted some freedom. I was also afraid that I would be sent to Dublin, like a lot of the girls who had nowhere to go after school, to do domestic duties in hospitals. That would mean more supervision by nuns and we were told they were very strict. My mother replied after a few months saying she was going to take me out soon and the rest of the letters would be a criticism of my spelling. I failed the Inter Cert so I was put into 5th year where about twelve of us were put into a class learning copy-typing while the others did science. I suppose it was thought that we might learn something we might use later, rather than trying to turn us into academics, which we were not.

CHAPTER 16

†††

Leaving the Orphanage and My New Life

One day the head nun called me and told me I was to leave the home. She told me I was going to live with my mother in London and that I was to go to Cork the next day with the matron to buy the suitcase. The suitcase was an important symbol of leaving the home. I had seen so many getting suitcases and keeping them under their beds until they finally said goodbye to us. At last my time had come.

I remember the pleasure of walking through Rushbrooke from the station with the large blue hard suitcase banging against the side of my leg, hoping that everyone who saw me knew that it meant I was going away. I was finally going to be like them. I placed the suitcase under the bed and spent the week collecting momentos from my friends and taking the case out and putting them inside it. Somehow they all seemed to find something to give to me, mostly holy pictures which had been cut out of Christmas cards with greetings on the back like *'In memory of the years we spent in Rushbrooke'* and *'God Bless You'* . During my last week an autograph book was sent around the study room and everyone signed it for me. Rhymes like *"When I'm dead bury me deep, place my books at my feet, tell the teacher I've gone to rest, and I won't be back for the next school test"*.were all over it and I still have this book and look through it for time to time. I often wrote to my friends there, but as they never had the price of a stamp they rarely replied. If they sent it through Sister she would read it and that was no use.

The suitcase packed with my nightie and shoes I had got for Christmas and a new tube of toothpaste and soap and I was ready to leave. The night before, Sister called for me to go to the parlour. I expected the call as I had seen others summoned. They had never told us what had happened at this meeting as they had been warned not to, but we had a good idea it was a talk about boys. Sister sat at the big round polished table with a big book opened at the centre. She told me to sit down opposite her and I perched myself nervously at the edge of the chair. I tried a smile at her but her expression showed no signs of familiarity. This was not going to be easy. "Your mother is taking you and you are going out into the big wide world. There's nothing I have to say to you only that if you stay away from boys you will never get into any trouble. Do you have any questions?". The tone of her voice sent any questions I might ever had had out of my head and I replied that I had none. She snapped book shut and told me I may leave.

Outside my friends were dying to know what had happened but there was nothing to tell. I was none the wiser for my interview. My friend from the orphanage who is older than me told me later years how disappointed she was when she finally lost her virginity. Sister had told her that a man was like a strip light and a woman the socket and that one fitted into the other. My friend expected her partner to be shaped a little differently.and her sex life to be more electrifying.

On the day I left I had to clean the dormitory as usual and then the matron asked me to get my friend Peggy back into bed as she was sick and the doctor was due to visit. Before the doctor arrived, the matron came in and asked Peggy where the pain was. She pointed to her side and Matron slapped her across the face and told her to tell the truth as she had the pain in a different place each time she was asked. Peggy cried and I asked her why she always gave different answers. She said that the pains kept moving around. My mother came to collect me so I had to leave. Peggy died four months later of Leukaemia at the age of fifteen .

The home was very quiet when I was leaving because of the doctor's visit. There was a cold atmosphere and when my mother arrived in the taxi with Jim, my stepfather, I had no time to say goodbye to my friends. I wanted to say good bye to Marion who had shared her pocket money with me, Angela who had sat and slept and lined up beside me for the past sixteen years and Patsy who was the most intelligent of the five of us and who had let us copy her homework. The matron called my name, I came downstairs, was handed my suitcase and sat into the back of the taxi next to my mother. I felt no emotion until Sister Dominic, who had taught me in Primary school and who was the church organist, rushed out from the church to wave to me. There were tears in her eyes and all of a sudden I started to cry. I was leaving the security of the home and going away with people I didn't know. I wanted to leave but I was nervous at the prospect of my new life. 'This is going to be great', I convinced myself. If only one of the others had been able to come away too. I needed the comfort of someone familiar. The two people in the taxi with me may have been my parents, but what would they be like to live with? I had no idea. The journey to Cork was spent in silence.

We went to the Woburn guest house, just like when I was eleven, and took off into the shops in the afternoon. I thought we were going shopping for me. I kept picking up bits and pieces in Woolworths and showing them to her, but my mother didn't take the hint. By the time I got back to the Woburn I was convinced I didn't want to go to London. I had suddenly become scared of everything. I was told to watch television in the lounge while my mother and Jim went into the bar, and when they had gone out to another pub I ran to the 'phone to ring Sister. I begged her to tell my mother to let me go back to the home, but she said she couldn't stop my mother from taking me. I cried and cried on the 'phone but it was no use.

We went to England next morning on the ferry. The 4th July 1971 was a beautiful day with blue skies and hot sun. I met Phyllis who was working on the ferry for the summer. She had left the orphanage two years before and was attending UCC. This was a unique achievement for one of us. She got four honours in the Leaving Cert and was entitled to a grant. She told me she had buried herself in books to block out what was going on in the orphanage around her. It had the opposite effect on me. I couldn't concentrate as I was always too conscious of what was going on and I wasn't particularly interested in studying anyway.

Phyliss asked me to go on the staff deck later to talk to her, so I told my mother where I was going. An hour later my name was called over the loudspeaker saying I was lost. I nearly died with embarrassment. My mother said she was afraid I would fall over the side and that she had to keep an eye on me as I had been in the orphanage for so long. She was treating me like a six-year old and kept holding on to my hand.

Our arrival at the flat in St. Mary's Road, Peckham, was at around midnight. I was fascinated with the huge houses in the road. Our one had five floors and we were in the basement. The flat was dark as the windows were small and the view out was a ledge of grass. There was a front room where I slept on the bed-settee, a small kitchen, a bathroom and my mother and Jim had the bedroom. Every night I had to wait until they finished drinking and.smoking before I could get into bed. The room always smelled of whiskey and beer and cigarettes.

My mother took a week off work to bring me around to various employment agencies to find work for me as a copy typist. I got a job typing out insurance claims in a big typing pool with twenty women in one room. I didn't smoke at that time and I found the smoke in the office made me feel ill. I found it difficult to mix with the other women who were older than me and didn't make any effort to make me feel welcome.

I never had a change of clothes like the others who seemed to have a different outfit every day. I also was embarrassed at my inability to spell. The copy typing was done from hand-written documents which were difficult to read, so I think I annoyed them asking how to spell the words all the time. Eventually I tried to work them out for myself which took a long time and so I wasn't as productive as the others. Work was often sent back to me with mistakes so I avoided all of this by taking half days off. I would walk around London rather than go home as Jim often had half days from the school in which he was teaching. I got £11 a week from my job and my mother took £7 for my keep, which left me with very little for clothes after I had paid my fares to work on the tube and for my lunches.

My mother used to open my mail, just like Sister in the home. She would never let me go for a walk on my own and always wanted to know where I wanted to go and why. She would tell Jim to go with with me, and, as always, Jim would do as he was told. The first time I asked her where the Catholic church was she told me I didn't have to go to Mass, now that I was no longer in the home. I said I wanted to go, which I did, and she showed me where the church was, just five minutes away from the flat. Still, she was always standing at the gate when I got back. If mass went on late I raced home to avoid interrogation as she always made me feel as if I was doing something wrong. She reminded me so much of Matron. Things were no better for me with her and.here I had no-one to talk to. I missed my friends in the home.

As the weeks went by I discovered our neighbours on the ground floor were nice to talk to. My mother was friendly with them so she allowed me to talk to them in the garden. Frank and Billy were brothers who had come from Australia years back. They spent a lot of time in the garden throwing a hatchet at a tree and pulling it out again. They cut the grass and weeded a small flower bed which had primroses, marigolds and sweet williams.

My mother used to tell me to go out and talk to them. Frank was at home a lot during the day and Billy was often out. Frank had a sports car and Billy had a big Volvo estate. For people who didn't appear to work they seemed to live well. I wondered where they got their money and I noticed them with keys one day and a big ball of putty. I asked them what they were doing and they told me they were making spare copies of keys. I didn't dare ask why, but I do remember asking where Billy was one day and Frank said he was in prison for a few days. Ask no questions.

When I knew them for a few weeks Frank would take me out at night to see the sights. We would go for a meal, usually for a pizza, and then drive to the West End to see the shops. I liked being with Frank and he was more like a father figure than Jim as I could talk to him and we had fun together. One night when we were parked in Battersea Park looking at the river, Frank kissed me on the lips. I didn't get nervous as I didn't expect anything else to happen and I liked being kissed. He held me close and I felt warm and safe. It was the first time I ever remember being held so tightly and I wanted to stay wrapped up. Nothing else happened that night and we went out several times after that. One night my mother walked in on us in his flat when we were kissing and she said I wasn't to go to his flat any more. Looking back I wondered how she ever let me go out with him at all, as she was so strict in other ways. I was now tied to the flat again and had lost the only person I could talk to.

We had a routine in the flat so we could all get to work on time. My mother was the first to wash and leave for work in the mornings. I would then wash and Jim was last. One morning while I was washing in the bathroom Jim opened the door (there was no lock) and apologised for the intrusion. As there was frosted glass in the door there was no reason for him to think the bathroom was free so when he did it a second time I knew something was wrong. I got my things together and went into the living room to dress. I was still in my nightie when he opened the door. He stood there in his pyjama bottoms. I asked him what he was doing and he replied "show me your beauty". I was scared and ran out into the toilet which was in the hall. I didn't leave the toilet until I heard him going out the front door.

Before going work I went to where my mother was working and told her what had happened. She left the office and we went to where Jim worked and brought him home in the taxi with us. She told me to repeat what I had told her and she asked him if it was true. He didn't deny it and she told him she would send him back to his sister in Accrington if he ever did it again. She was tough and he knew she meant it and he obviously didn't mind her domineering attitude. There was no apology, no sympathy for me, but it never happened again. From then on I made sure I was gone to work before my mother and I decided that one way or another I was going to get away from them.

I had always thought that nursing would be a lovely career, but never considered becoming a nurse as I was stupid and my exam results were poor. Still, as my life in the flat became more miserable, I thought it was worth a try so I sent lots of applications for nursing to various hospitals. Guy's hospital replied and an interview followed. I was particularly pleased when I read on the application form that I would have to live in. I might yet get out of this awful flat.

I was called for an interview in October 1971. I had turned the two Es on my Inter Cert into two Bs so that gave me an overall pass. I was very nervous going for the interview. I had rung my friend and confidante Father O'Connor the night before for advice. He had always found the right words for me when I lived in the home and he didn't let me down this time either. He told me to speak up for myself and to remember I was as good as the next person.

My mother came with me to the interview, but I was glad when she was asked to wait outside the office as she would have wanted to speak for me and I was ashamed of how fat she was - she was sixteen stone and walked with a stick, though she was only in her late forties. The matron asked me why I wanted to do nursing. I said I always wanted to look after people and that I couldn't do anything else. I knew I didn't sound genuine. After a while I found myself telling her about my mother, Jim and my childhood. I asked her to give me a chance as I wanted so much to leave home. She agreed to take me on a trial basis.

I couldn't believe it when I got a letter asking me to start that November. I rang Sister and Father O' and they were delighted. Sister had often said I would make a good nurse, though I didn't believe her. I used to think she wanted me to be a nurse as she was one.

CHAPTER 17

†††

Nursing - a New Start

On the day I was due to move to the nurses home, my mother asked Frank, our neighbour, to take me there in his car. The woman in charge of settling the new recruits thought Frank was my father and I was quite pleased to have a father with me.

I cried when Frank left me in my room as I was nervous of meeting the other girls. I didn't know what I was going to tell them about myself. I was sure they would sense I was different to them.

One of the girls knocked at my door to tell me that we were all to meet in the sitting room. I was the only Irish girl amongst them. I couldn't understand a word they said and they kept telling me to speak slower. I now had another problem - communication. I asked a black girl called Tara what tribe she came from. Everyone laughed. I thought that all black people came from tribes.

I kept myself in my room quite a lot, rather than mix with the others. They wore make-up and perfume, all I had was soap and toothpaste. For the first month in class I had to borrow paper, as my mother had not given me any money. I had to wait until I got paid. It was a great thrill for me to have my own money for my books. I picked copies with nice colourful covers and loads of pencils and biros. Just like the Outside Girls back in Rushbrooke.

I was very lonely in my bedroom. Compared to eighteen in a dormitory this was like solitary confinement. The girls went to the local pub at night and it was weeks before I allowed myself to be nagged into joining them. Grapefruit juice was to be my drink for the next few months; I was afraid to try alcohol. I could remember the smell of my mother when I was on holiday with her all those years ago when I was eleven and I didn't want to smell like her.

The second month I was there Frank came and took me to Bournemouth for the week-end. I was thrilled to see him. I hadn't seen my mother for two months and I was glad someone had come to visit me. The other girls had been going home for the week-ends and had come back talking about what they had done. It was just like being back at school. But this weekend was different.

When we arrived in Bournemouth we went into a flat owned by a friend of Franks. I innocently asked Frank where I was to sleep as there was only one bedroom with a double bed. He said I could have the bed and he would sleep on the settee. I was nervous going to bed though I didn't know why. I was lying trying to get to sleep when Frank came in beside me. He began to kiss and touch me. Even though I was afraid, I knew Frank would not hurt me; he had been so kind to me since I came to London. Then he moved on top of me and pushed my legs open. I still didn't know what he was going to do. I was afraid if he pressed his tummy too hard I would get pregnant. When he penetrated me I thought he was trying to kill me. I roared out and he put his lips to mine to quieten me. It hurt and when I got out of bed the sheets were soiled with blood. I was very embarrassed about the blood. I had a bath and Frank changed the sheets. He cuddled me for the rest of the night.

The second night I assumed that making love was all part of what was expected of me in return for the weekend away so we made love again. I was still very sore but was afraid to tell him in case he would reject me and bring me back to the nurses home. I wanted to stay with him and be looked after and held in this way. He said he would marry me when I was twenty-one. I was delighted to hear this as I just wanted someone to take care of me and I trusted him. He knew what he was doing and I didn't, so I let everything take its course. At that time I didn't think I could ever take care of myself. Frank was forty-five years old and I was grateful for his affection. He took me back to the nurses home that Sunday and that was the last I ever saw of him. He moved away from his flat and every time I thought of him I cried. I missed him. I felt very unsettled and withdrew into myself, talking to people only when I had to. I stayed in at night and seemed to be tired all the time.

Missing Frank brought back all my feelings of loneliness for the home in Rushbrooke. I missed my friends and Sister, even though she had been cruel at times; she was still like a mother to me, or perhaps an aunt, whatever an aunt was supposed to be like. I took a trip to the home when I had my first bank holiday weekend off and I was glad to see everyone again. I felt at last that I had nothing to prove as I now had a job, and I liked cheering up the kids who were left behind, knowing how much it meant to them to have a visitor. I was treated like an adult, even by Matron who talked to me, asking questions about my nursing training and I found I was no longer afraid she would burst into a temper. I stayed in the home and came and went as I pleased. They seemed glad to see me and it really felt like going home. I went out a few times with Jerry the guitar teacher who came to the home on Friday nights to teach some of us. I had a soft spot for him and kept in contact with him up to the time he got married.

When I got back from Rushbrooke from one of those weekends there was a note under my door asking me to visit the matron in Guys Hospital. She was very understanding when she realised I wasn't settling in and she moved me to New Cross Hospital which was predominantly Irish staffed. In no time at all I was making friends with everyone. A group of us nurses used to go to the Harp Club which was a dance hall. This was where I had my first drink, a Babycham; after a few months I graduated to Port & Lemon.

Still I felt a certain loneliness in my own bedroom, despite the noise from the wooden floors below which reminded me of the orphanage. Once I dreamed I was locked in my room, and I ran out into the corridor where I woke up. I was expecting to see the corridor of the orphanage, but one of my friends came around the corner in her nurses uniform and I realised where I was. Another time I was asleep during the day after night duty and could hear the voices downstairs. They sounded like the children in the Reck and I woke up exhausted. I still have dreams about Sister chasing me down the corridor. I always wake up before she catches me.

I didn't like working on the children's wards as I couldn't stand listening to a child crying. I had heard enough young children crying in the orphanage and it upset me. I thought the ward sister would give out to me if they cried.

Domestic duties on the ward were easy for me. My training in bedmaking from the orphanage stood to me. I loved making beds and even became annoyed if one of the patients sat on a bed afterwards. It spoiled my work of art. The routines and habits from the home are still with me today. I still peg clothes on the line with perfect spacing between them and if anyone else does the job I find myself re-doing it to my satisfaction. I lay the fire in the same way as the home, with each little piece of coal in perfect positioning. In the kitchen I always wash the cups first, and pots last, always pack shopping neatly and with items sorted as I go along. These are mostly good habits, but I know I am too much of a perfectionist in the way I do them. I can't do them any other way.

I found studying for nursing the most difficult as I had not done Biology at school. I was reading books that I could not understand and didn't ask anyone for help in case they thought me stupid. One day in class I was sent to get some Fallopian tubes in the lab next door. I didn't know what they were so I couldn't find them and went around the wards asking for some. I didn't realise they were in a jar in the lab.. Everyone was laughing when I got back.

One of the nursing tutors, Sister Arnell, was Irish and she was very strict. We were all afraid of her; we were told she had been trained in the army and we could see why. She would shout at us if we couldn't diagnose correctly or if the technique of applying a dressing was incorrect. As I had never had to make a decision before, I found diagnosis very difficult. I avoided any form of decision-making and would run to the toilet when I saw Sister Arnell approaching the ward. One morning when I dodged going on ward duty and hadn't reported to sick bay she came to my door. I cried when she told me to get to work and I told her her I wanted to give up nursing. I told her my whole story and that I felt I knew nothing and couldn't keep up with the class. Three times I handed in my notice to quit and three times the matron gave it to Sister Arnell who made me retract it. She kept pushing me until the end.

When the results of our final exams were put up on the board in the nurses home, I stood at the back. I was sure I had failed. Sister Arnell took me by the hand and stood me in front of the board. I had passed. I don't know who was more pleased, her or me. She said "Now Drennan, you can do whatever you want." It was the first thing I had achieved on my own in my life. I had proved to myself I could do something constructive. It was a great moment. I rang Father O'Connor and Sister and then the staff of the pathology laboratory who took me for a drink.

During my three years at New Cross hospital I had numerous affairs. As we went to the Harp Club regularly I got to know a lot of men. I didn't understand about relationships so I thought when a man asked you home, you went to bed with him. If someone said goodnight and that they would see me another night, I couldn't understand why he didn't want to make love to me that night. I would be very disappointed. I felt I wasn't good looking enough! I never classed myself as being attractive.

After a couple of months in New Cross I bought a doll in Woolworths and made a bed for it in the bottom drawer. I made a nightdress out of a hospital pillow case for the doll and would put it on each night before going to bed. It meant a lot to me to have my own doll. In the orphanage we shared dolls; they were never our own. I would close the drawer during the day in case the cleaner saw it and looked forward to opening it again when I got back to my room.

I was very much liked around the hospital. I was known as the Mad Irish Girl and was full of fun and always singing Irish songs at the top of my voice, especially on the geriatric wards where I was most at ease. I would love to sit down and talk to the patients - I was now gaining confidence in myself. I was still very shy about my body. My uniform and apron covered me well. I didn't like my breasts sticking out, even still. I was very slim and 5'6" tall.

While I was on the male orthopaedic ward a patient called Graham took a fancy to me. He was for ever asking me to talk and look after him. When one of the other nurses was assigned to give him a bed bath he sulked when we refused to change duties. When he got out of hospital he was invited to one of our nurses parties by a friend of mine as he had persuaded her to match us up. I danced with him a lot but was also attracted to Paul, a male nurse I worked with. After the party I told Graham to wait in my room while I helped to clear up. I went off with a few of the others, including Paul, to one of their rooms and listened to music until three in the morning. I had completely forgotten about Graham in my room and when I returned there he was standing very annoyed and left in a huff. That was the end of that infatuation. My relationship with the male nurse continued for quite a while. He carried a bleep with him in case he was needed on the wards. One night the bleep went off at 3 am. It made a loud noise and all the other girls knew he was with me. I got some slagging next morning.

I found it hard to say no to men. I didn't want to upset them. I used to think they wanted me for myself not just for sex. I wanted everyone to like me. I became more out-going and mixed well with everyone. I used to sing in the Irish pubs and do a bit of Irish dancing on the stage with a ceili band which used to play in Brixton. I enjoyed myself but still I felt people were looking at me and that I was different to them.

Once I qualified I was ready to move on . I wanted to get away from the institutionalised atmosphere of the nurses home with its warden who checked what time we came in and who made sure we didn't bring anyone home with us. I was now confident enough to look for another job and nearly ready to live alone. But not quite. My friend Myles who was a hospital porter and his wife offered to rent me a room in their house while I looked for agency work. This would give me more money and I liked the idea of working in different places. Lily was more like a mother to me than my own ever was. Every day she would have dinner ready for me and when I found a job Myles would drop me to work. This was a good arrangement which lasted for about six months until Myles introduced me to John.

John was dark handsome and shy. I met him in Guys hospital where he was a driver and was immediately attracted to his Spanish looks. His mother was Spanish and his father German and he lived with them and his brother. His father had been a sea captain and was away in Norway at the time. I fell in love with John very quickly and he asked me to move in with his family. It seemed practical, as my work was close-by in Kensington. His mother and he were very close and she was wary of me. I felt she liked me but resented my intrusion and the time she was losing with her son who was now aged 24. My living in the house was probably the better alternative to him moving out of home. A few months later I became pregnant. I continued to work at the hospital on day duty so I could go out with John at night, usually to friends houses and sometimes to John's hospital club room. I was very happy and loved meeting his friends though I was still a little shy with strangers at this stage.

I felt I had a friend in John but still I kept in close contact with Sister and some of the older girls in Rushbrooke. I used to go to stay in the orphanage whenever I had a long weekend and I loved seeing the other children. Sister would allow me to take them out for the day in a car which I would hire. One year I brought a small tent from England and took the children to the strand at Garryvoe. We set up the tent and the fun we had with the kids running in and out of it was wonderful. They had never experienced anything like it. I knew they would enjoy it. We bought bags of sweets and biscuits to eat while we drove around in the car. At one stage the kids became thirsty so we stopped the car outside someone's house and stole a bottle of milk. We drove away like gangsters which the kids thought was a great thrill.

When I was three months pregnant I took one of my trips to Cobh and told Father O'Connor my news. He asked me if I loved John and when I told him I didn't know, he told me not to marry him unless I was sure. I went back to London and when I was five months gone I married John. I still wasn't sure if I loved him, but my fear was that I would have to tell the nuns I was pregnant and unmarried. I was so much in touch with them they knew all about me and I still looked on them as my family. I felt secure when I was in contact with them, I still craved their approval and feared their disappointment in me. It's hard to describe the mixed feelings I had about the orphanage at this stage. I had spent so much time there that I couldn't cut loose. They were my only real family, and when I returned there I enjoyed the freedom of being able to come and go as I pleased.

Sometimes I walked around the dormitories and in my mind could hear the screams of the children when they were being punished and the matrons voice bellowing out, but as time went by the voices disappeared and some of my fears with them. I also felt a certain sympathy for the kids who were still there and gave them small treats which I hoped would brighten their days. One Christmas I brought stockings for the ends of their beds, remembering how little I used to receive from the tree downstairs. I taped the stockings on the ends of the beds and Sister told me to remove them. I cajoled her into leaving them there, which was just as well, because when I tried to remove one of them the paint on the bed came away with the tape.

I still had this need to please Sister and still just wanted her to say 'well done!'. When Karen was born I rang and told her the news. She wasn't fooled. She worked out my dates and told me she was very disappointed in me and that I should be ashamed of myself. Even though she didn't say it I could hear her voice in my mind like so many years before saying "You're no good, you are a bad egg, you will be just like your mother!" I felt I had let her down, I also felt hurt as my success in the exams seemed irrelevant and I was back to feeling worthless again.

John was a Catholic so we got married in the Church of the Seven Dolours in Peckham. It was a nice ceremony. One of my friends from the orphanage was my Maid of Honour. She was already married and living in Essex and I had kept in touch with her. I was bridesmaid to her and she and her husband often invited me for weekends while I was training at New Cross. They were always there for me when I needed a shoulder to cry on and we are still good friends.

My mother came to my wedding and Jim, her husband, gave me away. My mother arranged everything and spent the day acting the perfect hostess. This annoyed me as I just wanted things to roll along and for everyone to be relaxed. My mother kept organising people to sing and dance and was drinking a lot. She was so wrapped up in the festivities that we left her at it and slipped away as soon as we could. I rang Sister in the home to tell her how things went and she was happy for me.

Our honeymoon was spent in the Belgravia Hotel in Victoria and it lasted one night. We watched television in bed and John fell asleep. Not quite the honeymoon I had read about in My Weekly. We got up next morning and I went down to breakfast in the long evening dress I had bought for my wedding day. We spent the day moving into a flat of our own, still wearing the long dress. Our new home had a sitting room, bunk beds and a tiny kitchen with a two ringed cooker.

Life went on fairly normally and Karen was eventually born. I was two weeks overdue and the labour was induced. It was nothing like I had hoped, which was for a natural birth with John by my side. Karen was delivered by forceps and John was not allowed to stay with me. When it was all over I expected a doll-like bundle to be put in my arms, but what I saw was something resembling a monkey. I knew I loved her, but I was almost embarrassed to show her to anyone. She had jet black greasy hair and a round fat red face. My motherly instinct had yet to surface.

The second person to see me and my new baby after John was the matron from the orphanage who was living in London while training as a nurse in Guys hospital, and who I had kept informed of my condition. I used to ring her as Father O'Connor had asked me to keep an eye on her for his sake. He explained that she herself had been institutionalised since she was in the home as a child of about twelve and she would need a friend. This was difficult for me as I still felt a lot of anger towards her; she been responsible for a lot of the fear I felt while living in the orphanage and I always thought of her as the last person I would ever spend time with. I also felt a certain guilt in relation to my friends in the orphanage. I felt they would think I had betrayed them to be friendly with Matron after all they had suffered by her. However, I was now married and quite happy and had started to resolve some of the pain I felt about my childhood. As time went by I felt sorry for her as she had no-one of her own. In 1975 she had been finally asked to leave as a result of some enquiries made as to why some of the orphanage children had run away. She was now alone in London and here she was, coming to see my new baby.

Her visit to me in hospital was full of tension. I was ashamed of my ugly duckling and I thought she would look at her and think that this is exactly what I deserved. When she came into the ward she went straight over to the cot and said 'what a lovely baby!'. I knew she couldn't mean it. I also didn't want her to hold my baby after what I had seen her do to some of them in the orphanage. Floods of memories came back to me of her shaking children to stop them crying and shouting at them to shut up. She left the ward after the usual pleasantries and I was relieved it was all over.

John was delighted with Karen and we settled into family life with ease. We used to walk to Battersea Park on a Sunday afternoon. I wanted people to look at us and think 'what a lovely happy family' though I'm quite sure no-one even noticed us. I was happy in the knowledge that at last I fitted into normal society..

The flat was quite adequate, though it was probably strange to have a baby sleeping in a drawer. This was the large storage drawer under the bunks which we pulled out when she was in it. As time went by I found the flat depressing with John at work during the week with nothing to do but look after the baby. Most of the houses in the street were bedsits so there were very few small children and as a result I didn't meet any other mothers.

My weekly visits to the baby clinic were not as social as I expected as I still felt I was different to other mothers because of my background. It was quite a 'yuppie' area and everyone was in smart clothes and speaking with a posh accent and seemed to know each other. I still had an Irish accent and I wore chain-store cotton dresses and jeans. I didn't want to intrude or get to know them if I was going to appear different, so I just kept to myself. Also I knew it would only be a matter of time before they would realise where I came from. I felt sure that this would lead to rejection and I couldn't face that.

Mary, a friend of mine from the orphanage came to London to do Nursing and stayed with us for a few weeks. I took this opportunity to go back on night duty. I was only back at work a few weeks when I was pregnant again. While I was pregnant with Christine I became very depressed. I was working nights and looking after Karen during the day, getting very little sleep. I started to snap at John when he came home from work. He wanted his dinner ready and his shirts ironed. I failed to do both and John often came home to beans on toast. As for the ironing, he learnt that skill very quickly. I had no energy for anything other than looking after Karen, and not even enough for that.

I found it very lonely going to work leaving Karen, especially as I was full of guilt as I felt I hadn't looked after her properly during the day. I usually got about three broken hours of sleep so I would get up feeling very aggressive towards her. There were times when I caught myself shaking her to stop her crying. I was shocked when I realised I was doing exactly what I had been so horrified at the matron doing. All my little daughter wanted was to play.

I worked until I was eight months pregnant. Karen was now one year old and I liked working and being away from John at night. I didn't know then that sex was safe during pregnancy and that John was probably frustrated and this was part of our problem. Neither of us mentioned it as we were both as naive as one another.

The council got us a flat in Rotherhithe in south east London. We had applied for a change, as our own one was now too small for us. We were given a post-war mobile home known as a pre-fab. There were nine other families on this site off the main road. I now had my own garden for Karen to play in which was great and two other families had small children as well. I soon got to know them and we shared babysitting. I tried hard to mix with them but they were rough and not very clean. I was neat and tidy with a place for everything and everything in its place; the airing cupboard had to be neat and tidy so I could put my finger on what I wanted at any time. My neighbours seemed to have clothes strewn all over the place. I would have been ashamed if anyone walked in and saw my house untidy, they didn't seem to care about anyone else. I had been brought up differently, so it wasn't long before I kept myself to myself again.

During the last months of my pregnancy I got very depressed. John was coming home later and later and our relationship deteriorated and when Christine was born John missed the birth. However, the birth was beautiful and I immediately bonded with my new daughter. That was a Saturday. He came to see me that evening' evening visits were for fathers only. It was Wednesday again before I saw John. He came in all dressed up. I asked why he was so dressed up and he said he was going to the pictures with his brother. "Dressed like that?", I said, and he told me there was a nurse who kept chasing him and he was only taking her to the pictures to get her off his back. I remember shouting at him to get out. A nurse came in and asked him to leave as I was so upset. I spent another four days in the hospital and he never came to see me. A friend at the hospital took me home. John never really took to Christine, she had spoiled his plans to educate and give Karen everything. He wasn't ready for this extra commitment. It is only in recent months that they have become friends.

I never really recovered from John's lack of interest in Christine. As the months went by we had very little communication. Sex for me was painful and I made an appointment with a gynaecologist. He referred me to a psychiatrist who after a few sessions discovered that the pain I was experiencing was related to my poor relationship with John. My pain was an attempt to avoid sex with John and showed up the state of our marriage. He recommended a marriage counsellor, but John didn't accept that he had anything to do with my problem. He refused to go.

We existed under the same roof, sleeping in separate rooms, I with Christine, John with Karen, but going out together as if there was nothing wrong. John enrolled Karen in an expensive private kindergarten (where Princess Diana used to work). I resented this as John didn't consult me and it meant I was stuck with having to work extra days to finance it. He was determined that Karen should have the best of everything no matter what the cost. I would have preferred to buy books and nice toys and not have to worry about keeping up appearances. John won the argument so I changed jobs to work as an ambulance driver. This meant I could drop Karen to the kindergarten and Christine to the nursery near the ambulance station. This routine continued for over a year.

I was often late collecting Karen as the job hours could not always be consistent. Karen would cry if I was late (she didn't seem happy in the kindergarten anyway) and the money I was earning was not as good as I expected. I threatened to remove Karen to another nursery and John counter-threatened that if I did he would leave me. When the new term fee was due to be paid I decided it was time to stop. John did as he promised and after a heated argument I packed his bags and he left.

We tried to get back together but we were no longer compatible. I moved into a three bedroomed maisonette when the prefabs were demolished and hoped that the move would encourage a reconciliation. It was not to be and we divorced two years later. John wanted custody of the children and was sure he would win when he revealed by background to the court. At home he had started to taunt me saying I should have stayed in the orphanage and should go back there. In court, however, my background was not seen as any disadvantage to what they saw was a good mother. I got custody of the children with John allowed access every Sunday.

For the next two years I was lonely and depressed. I did and didn't want John. I wasn't happy alone but I was confused as to what I wanted. All my insecurities returned and I withdrew into myself. I didn't want to see anyone or to have anyone see me. I wore the same clothes all the time, completely disinterested in the passing fashions. I lived in black corduroy jeans with a sloppy t-shirt over them and I let the house get untidy and disorganised. I kept the curtains pulled and didn't notice the dirt.

I came to my senses one day when my friend Monica visited me from out of town. I removed a pile of laundry from the settee and asked her to sit down and she sat on the arm of the chair to avoid getting dog hairs on her suit. She told me the place was a mess and asked what was wrong. I realised what I was living in and felt embarrassed. She advised me to contact a social worker who advised me to have Karen taken into care for a while. This was a shock to me as I didn't realise I could be affecting the children. It had occurred to me that they might be better off back in my old orphanage for a while but the thought of being without them and them missing me made me determined that my children wouldn't suffer. I decided I should do something for myself. I got a neighbour to come and help me to tidy up my house and, though she was surprised to be asked, she agreed without hesitation. She became a good friend. From that time on.I depended on Carol when I was down and slowly my depression lifted.

The next eight years were spent in this house and I was very happy there. I had other good neighbours and living on my own gave me confidence and finally the ability to make decisions. This suited me as I felt in control of my own life at last. The children went to nursery and later school, and I stayed at home and did childminding while I was on the dole. This was the first time I was on the dole and I didn't like it, but if I had gone out to work my childminding expenses would have been too high. I got various other benefits as I was on the dole and my childminding money paid for small luxuries like toys for the kids and doing up the house. My life was full as I had renewed friendships with some of my nursing colleagues from Guys and we used to go to the Irish clubs around London. I was growing in confidence and, as I had no-one to answer to, felt a freedom that suited me very well.

I was finding my feet at last, but still there was something missing. A man perhaps? I made friends with other mums at the children's school. Six of us divorced mums would go out together to a jazz pub on a Saturday night where we got to know a nice group of lads. This growing circle of friends led to various relationships. I seemed to be attracted to artistic types who drifted in and out of my life at various times. The group in the pub included policemen from the local station. It was in this pub that I met the man I had my first affair with since John.

I stayed drinking late in the pub one night and so did Michael. That was the start of a very good relationship. Michael was a policeman on the local beat. He was already married twice and he and his present wife had two children. He didn't want to break up the family and I understood this. I would not like to have been a home wrecker and I was happy in my own life without any commitment. We enjoyed each other's company and he often called to me on his way to work. We would just have a cup of tea and he would check that I was OK. He offered to give me money if ever I was short and fix the car and do any odd jobs in the house. We also had a physical relationship which was passionate and intense.

I had a deep affection for Michael and he was always in the background. However, I knew he was never going to be free and could never stay the night. I wanted to wake up with someone in the morning. Our relationship didn't tie me to him and I felt free to go out with anyone I chose, which I did with a series of men who attracted me in one way or another. I lived with a few of them for months at a time and the relationships ended for various reasons. I was always searching for some sort of stability, but always seemed to pick the wrong men, until I was introduced to Brian.

We met through a friend and he was a bit slow to chat in the beginning as it was only a few weeks since his wife had died. I immediately felt very sorry for him and asked him home for a cup of coffee. Brian sat in the living room and began to cry. I didn't know what to do so I just cuddled him and let him talk. His wife had died of breast cancer having been told just weeks beforehand that she would recover. They had had a happy twenty five years together and had just celebrated their anniversary before the news of her illness had broken. He was very lonely without her and this was the first night he had managed to face a visit to the pub. He had a married son and a daughter who was living with her boyfriend and he didn't want to dampen their happiness with his sorrow. Slowly our relationship built up with dinner out and more trips to the jazz clubs as Brian was very keen on music.

I found myself becoming comfortable in his company and he offered me a certain security I had never felt before. I started to spend less time with my other friends - Michael was still in the background and I didn't want to let him go. He had become part of my family and had been a good friend. I managed to keep him as a friend, but our physical relationship ended. Brian didn't put on any pressure, but Michael was still married and the best part of our relationship was our warmth and friendship which still fitted into the picture.

I wanted more time with Brian on our own and slowly it was convenient for him to stay the odd night as his workplace was nearby. His own house on the other side of London had a basement where his in-laws lived. They noticed his absence and when I visited the house during the day to help Brian to tidy it up, I could see his in-laws peeping through the curtains. His French daughter-in-law confronted me over a cup of coffee. She had assumed Brian and I had been having an affair while his wife was still alive. I still don't know if she believed me, but I was glad it was true.

That Christmas, six months after we met, I had all of his family to my house for dinner. I tried to make it as special as possible, as I had always done, with doilies and sweets and decorations just like we had in the orphanage. The day went well with everyone quite relaxed and eating and drinking their fill. The family appeared to have accepted me. His son was no trouble and he and his wife took to me straight away. His daughter wasn't quite as easy. Her boyfriend liked me, but she was wary of me and still is to this day. My children had taken immediately to Brian and loved his son, a newly-found brother. Not long after that I moved into Brian's house and we started to live as a couple, with all its domesticity. I gave up work as there was a lot to be done to the house to get it back into shape and convert rooms to accommodate everyone. It was lovely being a kept woman for a while with the independence of a car and plenty of money to buy whatever I needed. Brian's salary from the council was more than adequate for all our needs. Life was good.

Brian showed me other sides of life. He was group leader of

the Woodcraft Folk which was a mixed youth group similar to the scouts. He introduced me to Camping. There was to be a two-week trip to the Isle of Wight with three dozen kids aged from five to sixteen. I was delighted with the offer of a holiday and liked the idea of being with kids again, just like at the orphanage. I was hoping to help to give them a good time and enjoy their laughter and fun. I packed a large rigid suitcase full with shorts and sandals. That was my first mistake.

All the kids arrived with knapsacks filled with long leggings and waterproof gear. They knew what they were in for. I didn't. I didn't expect to have to wash in a tiny bowl with freezing cold water. I didn't expect to have to trample through briars to get to the bucket and toilet seat under a piece of canvass which served as our toilet for the weeks. I didn't expect to have my legs ripped with briar and nettles. I didn't expect to have to get up when a whistle blew and line up in front of my perfectly tidied tent for inspection. If this was a holiday, it wasn't my idea of one.

No matter what the weather we had to wear the uniform of the club which was a heavy green shirt which reminded me of the apartment cloths which were kept under the urine buckets in the orphanage. The heat was intense at times but we still had to wear the shirt tucked into our jeans and stay smart. We were the Woodcraft Folk, and *"Span the World with Peace"* was our motto.

I refused to go on a bivouac which would have entailed sleeping under the stars and cooking breakfast by rubbing twigs to start the fire. This was too much. Brian and I had our first falling out. I wanted to go home so he told me to do just that. I was to shape up or ship out. But there was nowhere to go. I was one of the drivers of the mini buses so I couldn't disappear. There was nothing to do but to get used to it and relax. I could be found hiding behind the tent sunbathing, but apart from that I kept in line. I enjoyed that sing-songs around the camp fire at night and the trips to the pub when all the kids were asleep. I was amazed at how much the kids enjoyed themselves, despite being away from home at such a young age. Some of them came from fairly deprived backgrounds, so I presume camping was better than what they were used to - a bit like when I was at the orphanage. I was amazed to realise that others had come from upper-class families, perhaps their parents got rid of them for a week or two. What was interesting was how they all mixed together so well with no evidence of 'haves and have-nots' for the week. Needless to say, I didn't venture out with the Woodcraft Folk again.

Not all Brian's treats were unsuccessful. I had a memorable weekend in Bath which corrected the balance. We stayed in a five-star hotel in a room called Carnation. The wallpaper had carnations with matching bedspread and curtains. Our bed was turned down at night and the lamps lit and everything tidied. I kept our wine cool in the bidet in the en-suite bathroom. I couldn't believe that when I used just half of the bubble bath that it was replaced with a full one a few hours later. There was loads of towels, a television, telephone and easy chairs and room service for snacks at night. This was living as I had never known it. Shortly after that we got engaged and married six months later.

Michael gave me away at my wedding which was held in Woolwich registry office and followed by a big reception in Brian's house. His friends did the catering and the party went on until about two in the morning. My friend Monica, one of the Outside Girls in the secondary school and who received my mothers letters for me, came to the wedding. She was only schoolfriend at the wedding as she was the only friend living in London at the time. We honeymooned in Paris for four days and returned to settle into married bliss. After lengthy discussions Brian finally agreed to another child. He wasn't too keen on the idea as he thought he was too old and thought a child would curtail our freedom. He gave in when I persisted and Katy was born after two miscarriages two years later. Katy is now the apple of Brian's eye and she has taken years off him. Katy goes to the local school and we lead a normal life in county Cork with my two daughters from my first marriage.

CHAPTER 18

†††

My Mother, My Sister and Uncle Alex

My mother came from a strong Protestant family in Whiteabbey, Co.Antrim. She had two brothers and one sister of whom she always spoke as if she was jealous. My mother never got on well with her own mother and always thought she favoured her sister. She loved her father and she was the apple of his eye. My birth was an accident. My mother says my father was a sailor whom she met in Belfast. There seems to be no reason why my birth should have been such a big secret, perhaps it was something to do with the fact that I had to be baptised a Catholic before I was admitted into the orphanage. My mother may have been afraid to reveal this to her staunchly Protestant respectable family at a time when relationships with Catholics were strictly forbidden. When Brian and I came to Ireland on holiday in 1988 I asked Brian about going to County Antrim to look up my mother's family. I still wanted to know more about where I came from, whether or not I had uncles and aunts. Miss Bullen had told me that I had a sister who was ten years older than me. My mother had denied it, but I didn't believe her and that made me want to know even more.

We made our way to Whiteabbey. I was excited and nervous though I was sure it was a waste of time. We went to a pub in Newtownabbey which is a Protestant area. Brian said he would do the talking, I couldn't understand why, after all I was Irish and he was English. I said to him "This is my country" "Not up here it's not" he replied. I went straight to the bar and asked the barwoman if she knew of any Drennans in the area. She said she didn't. We bought a drink and sat down. The barwoman spoke to a small group of men at another table. One of the men came over and he said knew a George Drennan years ago who was a postman. I didn't know I had an uncle, George, at that time so that wasn't any help. My mother had said that her family were

Protestant farmers, that she had twin brothers one of whom had died of measles at the age of four months, and that was all I had to go on.

We went to the Protestant vicar who told us he thought the Drennans had emigrated to Canada years before but that possibly some of his parishioners could help. We went back to London and a few months later he rang to say he had an address and a telephone number of an Alex Drennan in Canada. I was pregnant with Katie at the time so it was a while before I had the time and courage to make this contact.

When Katie was four months old we came to Ireland to live. We had bought a house in Aghada, County Cork, and planned to retire on Brian's pension.

I often visited the orphanage which was just about twenty miles away, and as the months went on I found myself getting depressed again. Seeing the children in the home brought back terrible memories and even though they were better cared for and appeared happy they triggered emotions in me that I was unable to cope with. I still hadn't resolved my childhood and felt that I needed to know who I was and where I came from. My mother had told me I would be better off not knowing about my family so it was with some hesitance that I made my next move to trace my relatives.

I rang Alex Drennan in Canada one day. Alex's wife answered the 'phone and I asked her if she was Drennan. When she said she was I asked her if her husband was one of a twin and then she asked me who I was. I told her I thought I was her husband's niece and that my name was Phil. She said that her husband already had a niece in Whiteabbey called Phyliss. I told her my mother's name was Elizabeth, but she was known in London as Betty. She said that she must have been Lily who she understood was dead for years. This was enough to convince her to get her husband to ring me back when he got home.

When Alex rang back he told me he was delighted to hear from me and wanted to know all about me. He was very upset that I had been in a home for seventeen years without him knowing. He didn't disbelieve anything I told him as he said my mother was the black sheep of the family. He told me I had a half sister called Phyliss who was born in 1943. This was ten years before I was born. My mother married Philip when she was nineteen and five months pregnant with my sister Phyllis and left Philip and Phyllis when she was just five. Nobody knew where she went. My sister was sent to Whiteabbey where she lived with our grandparents, Uncle Alex, Uncle George and Auntie Annie.

Uncle Alex asked me questions about my mother as he couldn't understand why she had left home and why she had later deserted her first daughter and then me. He was very sympathetic and said there would be great celebrations in Canada amongst my huge family that another member of the family had been discovered. I told him I wanted to find my sister and he advised me to get in touch with her son Ken who worked as a detective inspector in Belfast. Alex promised to come to see me soon and that was the end of that conversation and the start of a new life for me.

I left a message for Phyliss to ring me through her son and it was late that evening when she rang me. I hadn't moved from the telephone all day in anticipation. I didn't know what was going to be revealed and I was nervous and excited and full of great expectations of my new sister.

When she rang the first question she asked me was if I knew if our mother was alive. She had spent years looking for her in Ireland, but of course as my mother had remarried and moved to London, there was no trace of her. We cried together over the 'phone and exchanged news of our families. She had married, had three sons, one daughter and three grandchildren, and divorced, all by the age of forty five. There was a lot to catch up on so we made arrangements to meet. In the meantime I rang my mother and told her I had been in contact with my sister. I expected her to be shocked, but she just said "so what?". I gave her Phyliss's telephone number and when she seemed disinterested I called her a bitch. She hung up on me.

Waiting to meet Phyllis at the railway station in Dublin was a time of intense anticipation. I had clear images in my mind. I expected to see a tall slim figure, capable and reliable, glamourous and warm. What I saw arriving on the platform was a carbon copy of my mother: short and carrying a walking stick and dressed completely in black. My heart sank. I went towards her and we called each others names and put our arms around each other and cried. We went to a friends house nearby. Mary had been in the orphanage with me and was married with six children. She was one of three sisters who I remember coming into the home and being stood up on the table and stripped down. She coped well with her experience of the home and now was happily married with six children.

She put two mattresses on the floor in her dining room and when it was time to get into bed I undressed quickly while Phyliss was in the bathroom. She reminded me so much of our mother that I automatically turned to the wall while she was undressing, as I always had to do with my mother.We spent the night looking at photographs and catching up on our lost lives.

We told each other our stories and found we had a lot in common. From the photographs we could see that my daughter Christine was the image of her son David, we had both married when we were five months pregnant and we both loved talking. We also established that there was a Drennan nose common to all of us. Phyllis had done better in school than I had. She had been good at maths and got good results in her exams (unlike me) and had gone on to work in an accountants office. Her marriage had been happy for a few years but her husband had been involved in the northern troubles and had left to live in England. She had three sons who were, and still are, all working in the British Forces.

I suggested she make contact with my mother, although my mother had refused to phone Phyllis herself. My mother hadn't told Jim about her first daughter and wanted to do it in her own time. They eventually met and their reunion was successful . She is now much closer to my mother than I ever was. They are very alike and spend a lot of time together. Phyllis says she is still bitter about the lost years with our mother, but all she can see is a seventy one year old woman who is crippled with arthritis and who won't be around for much longer. I have been excluded from this cosy relationships and it hurts.

My mother never rings me directly. If she wants to know anything about me she rings Phyllis. I think she can't cope with the guilt which she still can't admit she feels. Phyllis is still living alone in Whiteabbey where she was brought up. We visit each other every year and we have good fun together and avoid talking about our mother as our feelings for her are different. Perhaps we will have more time for each other when I feel less angry about our mother.

Uncle Alex eventually rang to say he was coming. He arrived in Belfast airport and my mother was there to meet him. He landed with his wife, Eileen, their daughter Jill, her husband Stephen and their daughter Stephanie. This was quite a collection coming to meet their newly discovered cousin in Cork.

I had a lot of questions for Uncle Alex and he had some questions to ask my mother about me. Like why I was a Catholic, why had I been put into a Catholic orphanage and not given to the Salvation Army and indeed why I couldn't have been sent to them to look after. My mother put a lot of blame on her mother who she said told her not to bring me to Belfast. She said that when I was five, she told her mother that I was in an orphanage in Cork and that her mother told her to leave me there. Uncle Alex found that hard to believe, especially as she was a staunch Protestant and would have immediately taken me out of that alien atmosphere. My mother kept drinking whiskey and saying that I had been better off not knowing I had a half sister and that

I never loved her anyway and what was the point. She tried to shift the guilt onto me, but that didn't work. I was strong at this stage and this shocked her. She refused to tell me who my father was as she said he was probably happily married and didn't need me upsetting his life. At the end of two days I was none the wiser for all the talk. As well as all that, my mother still wouldn't admit she had done anything wrong, saying she did what was best for me at the time.

To this day this is still her stance. As recently as a few months ago, on a friend's advice I rang my mother and told her I loved her. My friend thought it might be the spur we needed to heal our wounds. I hoped he was right. When I rang her and told her how I felt about her she laughed at me and told me to pull the other one and slammed the phone down. I never tried again. I am still waiting to hear from her. I am also still trying to trace my father.